Organizations

Organizations

A Systems Approach

STEFAN KÜHL

Translated by
PHILIP SCHMITZ

LONDON AND NEW YORK

First published 2013 by Gower Publishing

Published 2016 by Routledge
2 Park Square, Milton Park, Abingdon, Oxon OX14 4RN
711 Third Avenue, New York, NY 10017, USA

Routledge is an imprint of the Taylor & Francis Group, an informa business

Gower Applied Business Research
Our programme provides leaders, practitioners, scholars and researchers with thought provoking, cutting edge books that combine conceptual insights, interdisciplinary rigour and practical relevance in key areas of business and management.

British Library Cataloguing in Publication Data
A catalogue record for this book is available from the British Library.

Library of Congress Cataloging-in-Publication Data
Kühl, Stefan.
    Organizations : a systems approach / by Stefan Kühl.
        pages cm
    Includes bibliographical references and index.
    ISBN 978-1-4724-1341-3 (pbk) -- ISBN 978-1-4724-1342-0 (ebk) --
    ISBN 978-1-4724-1343-7 (epub) 1. Organization. 2. Organizational sociology.
    I. Title.
    HM711.K84 2013
    302.3'5--dc23

                                                                            2013020846

ISBN 13: 978-1-4724-1341-3 (pbk)

CONTENTS

ABOUT THE AUTHOR

Stefan Kühl studied sociology and historical science at Bielefeld University, Johns Hopkins University in Baltimore, Université Paris-X-Nanterre, and the University of Oxford. He is a professor of sociology at Bielefeld University and works as an organizational consultant for Metaplan, a consultancy firm based in Princeton, Paris and Hamburg.

CHAPTER 1

ORGANIZATIONS: WHAT ARE THEY, ACTUALLY?

Although organizations define our lives to a significant degree, we never receive any training in how to deal with them. After all, no school curriculum in the world offers a course in "organizationology." Most courses of study prepare people for specific activities in companies, public administration, hospitals, or churches, while only peripherally touching on how to conduct oneself in such organizations. Even in disciplines such as sociology, economics, or psychology, frequently only the specialized course offerings provide information about the way organizations actually function. As a result, knowledge of the workings of organizations and how to behave in them is acquired only incidentally.

A person's first contact with an organization generally takes place immediately upon seeing the light of day. In the Western world, at least, people are born in hospitals. Homebirth is the exception, so that parents who elect this organizationally disassociated alternative generally have to justify the decision to their circle of acquaintances. Yet even parents who would like to spare their newborns an early encounter with an institution figure that, in an emergency, a hospital is able to provide a greater range of services than a midwife practicing on an outpatient basis. For that reason, they keep the telephone number of the nearest hospital close at hand.

Whereas the first two or three years of a child's life are by and large free of organizations, an intense contact lies ahead and is experienced as a distinct break. In kindergarten or elementary school, a child may initially perceive its teachers as individuals, but it quickly realizes that they are merely parts of a larger whole and are people who can be replaced. Children's behavior and expectations also clearly reflect that they have no question about the difference between a family setting and an organizational one. In the same sense, secondary schooling confronts us not only with the mathematical rule of three, the correct way to form a genitive, and the conditions that create terminal moraines, but simultaneously socializes us to proper behavior within organizations. Here, one can no longer rely on being treated as something special and receiving love regardless of performance, as one would in the parental home. Instead, students must learn that they are viewed from a very specific perspective and constantly compared with others. They learn that they are viewed primarily in the role of a pupil and realize that if they do not conform to certain rules, they face the threat of being expelled from the organization called "school" (Dreeben, 1980: 59ff.).

We gather our initial experiences with organizations in an "audience role," for example, as a kindergartner who needs to be amused, a pupil who requires instruction, or an adolescent who has been picked up by the police. Yet as we transition to adulthood, we increasingly find ourselves playing "achievement roles" in organizations. We become involved in school or university student unions, are compelled (in some countries, at least) to enter the military or perform civilian service and, last but not least, we begin our working lives in organizations. It is not unreasonable to suspect that in our times the transition from adolescence to adulthood is more clearly delineated by the assumption of an achievement role in an organization than by leaving home or founding a family of one's own.

Pursuing vocational activities in a business, government agency, church, school, or research facility seems such a matter of course to us that launching an independent career immediately after school or college appears to be a special path. People strike off on their own because they don't get along with superiors (which often means with organizations), because no organization is willing to pay them a satisfactory salary, or because they want to "do their own thing," without being controlled by managers or administrators. But even the self-employed, who often choose this path because they intuitively reject organizations or have been rejected *by* organizations, must later come to terms with small organizations of their own if their activities have brought them success.

As organizational scientist Chester Barnard (1938: 4) remarked in the 1930s, however, not only our work lives but also our leisure time is structured to a large extent by organizations. Bridge clubs, crochet groups, brotherhoods and student fraternities, extracurricular educational activities like continuing education programs or dance clubs, athletic associations, prayer circles, parent groups, citizens' initiatives and political parties offer further opportunities to join specific forms of organizations with pleasures and pathologies all their own. Glancing at a monthly bank statement is often enough to determine just how many dues-paying (although perhaps passive) memberships one holds.

Even at the end of life, abundant experience with organizations can still be gathered. Long before physical death occurs, people are generally removed from their achievement roles within organizations through retirement, termination or an unsuccessful bid at re-election. Oftentimes, they do not experience their removal as liberating but just the opposite, namely, as separation from key social reference points and social death. Yet early removal offers organizations the advantage that they can avoid having to cope with the all-too-abrupt personnel changes that physical death brings about. Naturally, it occasionally happens that people die while performing their achievement roles: a forester might be crushed by a falling tree, a manager could suffer a heart attack, or a soldier could be killed during a maneuver or in combat. But such events are classified as accidents which represent somewhat out-of-the-ordinary situations. In contrast to retirements or dismissals, organizations respond to them as crises. This explains why people normally experience the end of their lives—and this is strikingly reminiscent of early childhood—once again as more or less helpless members of the audience in terms of organizations. This extends from the care they receive in hospitals and the processing of their insurance claims, to having their bodies tactfully removed by a funeral company.

ORGANIZATIONAL DISASSOCIATION AS AN EXPRESSION OF EXCLUSION

Organizations dominate modern society to such a degree that being away from them even for short periods is considered unusual. A one-year trip around the world entails not only taking leave of family and friends, but also temporarily waiving contact with organizations. Indeed, that type of travel is often motivated by having received an "overdose" of organization during military service or the initial years of professional life. When the job title of "stay-at-home mother" or, in extremely rare cases, "stay-at-home father" comes up, say, on a quiz show or at a party, it is generally put forward with a mixture of defiance and embarrassment, which is an indication that organizationally disassociated roles of this kind require an explanation. As well, the isolation that these women and the small number of men report when they are reduced to this role can be explained through their lack of contact with organizations.

People who spend their entire lives—not just a period of time—without ever joining an organization may well be said to be living on "the margins of society." The person who never went to school, performed military service, or held a job, and still does not belong to any associations can justifiably be viewed as "excluded," to use a favored sociological term. If one examines the development of exclusion in the homeless, it generally begins with a loss of employment and then progresses to withdrawal from associations or resignation from a political party. At that point, contacts with organizations occur only very sporadically and generally under coercion, as might occur in connection with the police, and are perceived by the excluded individuals with growing irritation.

The modern welfare state, however, is geared to discouraging and preventing organizationally disassociated lives. While it might still be possible to "protect" the very young from organizations, it becomes difficult as soon as they reach the age of compulsory education. In most countries, avoiding compulsory education would require a substantial criminal effort on the part of the child's parents because, if necessary, compliance can be enforced by the police. Frequently, the parents' only alternative is to enroll their child in one of the "free" schools which are supposed to shun the typical features of organizations such as discipline and hierarchy. But as experiments at alternative schools like Summerhill in England and the Odenwaldschule in Germany have shown, the outcome is not an organization-free form of learning— the so-called de-schooling of society—but merely a different form of organization which is in part equally emotionally and physically stressful.

People who in the later phases of their life do not pursue professional activities in organizations are not by any means left entirely in peace. Instead, in that situation they are serviced by government employment offices that are sometimes caricatures of bureaucratic mechanisms. For these offices, reintegration into the workforce frequently means nothing more than the resumption of work activity in an organization. Making regular attempts to obtain a salaried position in an organization becomes the precondition for receiving financial support.

The prominence of organizations in modern society and the degree to which they define our lives raise the question of what these entities actually are.

Organizations: An Initial Approach

We are quick to use the word *organization*. In everyday speech we often use *organize* or *organization* simply to describe goal-directed, systematically regulated processes. We speak of organizing or organization when various, initially independent acts are put into a purposeful sequence, thereby achieving "rational results" (Weick, 1985: 11). It goes without saying that the organization of a children's birthday party falls under the bailiwick of the mothers and fathers concerned. We learn from our parents, grandparents, or great grandparents that during difficult times people occasionally had to organize things on the black market in order to survive. Meanwhile, all that lifts our spirits today is when a colleague organizes a round of drinks in a crowded bar in the blink of an eye. If too many goals are scored against an international soccer team, commentators begin to complain that the team's defense needs to be re-organized.

This broad understanding of organization underlies almost all forms of organizing wherever it is found. Societies organize their ways of living together communally, as do families. Groups organize evening card games, companies organize the most profitable way to manage their businesses, protest movements their demonstrations, and those who attempt suicide—with greater or lesser success—their "long way down" (Hornby, 2005). According to this view, even laws, traffic regulations, house rules, user manuals, restaurant menus, game rules and sheet music all appear to be an expression of organization.

Yet this understanding is poorly suited for more detailed analyses; ultimately, it denotes nothing more than an order which is utilized to accomplish something. The concept is formulated so broadly that in the end it encompasses everything that is in any way structured, regular, or goal directed.

In Support of a Narrow Definition of Organization

In contradistinction to this inflationary usage, it has become generally accepted in scientific circles—and especially in the system theory—to use the word organization to designate a particular form of social system which can be differentiated from other social systems like families, groups, networks, protest movements, or nation-states. Some of these specific systems even feature the "organization" label in their names as a means of denoting their particular nature. One need only think of the "O" in the World Health Organization (WHO), the North Atlantic Treaty Organization (NATO), the Organization of the Petroleum Exporting Countries (OPEC), and the Organization for Economic Co-operation and Development (OECD). Others do not use the word organization but rather synonyms such as the word institution, which now sounds somewhat dated but is still found in names like the Brookings Institution or the Smithsonian Institution. Today, self-respecting organizations tend to adorn themselves with the trendy concept of an "agency." As an illustration, in 2002 the US Ballistic Missile Defense Organization was renamed the Missile Defense Agency.

Other organizations use their names to designate the specific type of organization they represent, for instance, a business enterprise, public administration, church, association, political party, or army. In the case of the *Church* of Scientology, the Irish Republican *Army* or a Major League Baseball *Club* in the US, observers may find it debatable whether the organizations are justified in describing themselves as a church, a sports club, or an army, or whether they are actually businesses or criminal outfits. Nevertheless, it is virtually impossible to deny them their status as organizations. Many organizations do not explicitly mention the word in their names. General Electric, Daimler-Benz and France Télécom have every reason to believe that they can be unequivocally identified as organizations even though their names make no indication of it.

Naturally, cases repeatedly arise where we are not entirely certain whether we are dealing with an organization or not. Does a one-person company that bills itself as a marketing agency qualify as an organization? When nations assemble on an occasional basis to coordinate climate policies, does that warrant the use of the term *organization* in the narrower sense? Does a branch of a state university system represent an organization in itself, or is it only a geographically defined sub-division of the department of education? Of course, such borderline cases actually only sharpen our understanding of organizations.

The Development of Organizations in Modern Society

When we apply the narrower system theoretical definition of organizations, we see that they are a phenomenon that has only emerged over the last few centuries. To be sure, the construction of the Egyptian pyramids or the development of an extensive water-based economy in the Nile delta are impressive cases of "organization," but only in the broader sense of the term. At first glance, the initiation rites, hierarchies, and precise sets of regulations found in cloisters make them appear to be precursors to organizations, and yet they were more an expression of pre-modern societies. The affiliation of craftsmen into guilds and leagues in medieval cities might remind us of modern organizations, but these also tend to fall under the definition of an organization in the broader sense.

It is correct that rudimentary forms of membership in exchange for compensation have existed since ancient times. One need only think of the day workers who offered their labor in exchange for wages, or mercenaries who made their combat abilities available to the highest-paying military commander. However, until the emergence of the Modern Age, other forms of aggregating people predominated. Slave owners held their slaves as physical property. Feudal lords levied taxes on their serfs and exacted unpaid labor, imposing their demands through force if necessary. In the case of the guilds, one was born a member, so to speak. It went without saying that a son would follow in his father's trade and thereby also assume his membership in the guild. Membership did not involve an independent decision, but rested instead on birth.

One central characteristic of all these pre-modern forms of order is that they encompassed a person in his or her entirety. In highly simplified terms, the slaves who were used to build the pyramids or dig canals couldn't simply go home after work or quit their jobs at the Egyptian construction sites. Entering a cloister was a fundamental life decision with the effect that all of one's activities transpired within the framework of a communal Christian life. Guilds and leagues were not primarily institutions aimed at safeguarding monopolies, but additionally regulated their members' cultural, political, and legal relationships.

Organizations in the narrow sense of the word appear for the first time during the Modern Age with the development of bureaucratic administrations, the formation of standing armies consisting of professional soldiers, the rise of education in schools and universities, treatment of the sick in clinics or hospitals, the creation of penal institutions, the transfer of production to factories and manufacturing plants, and the founding of associations, federations, unions, and political parties. It was only after such organizations had formed that it increasingly became the norm for membership to be the result of a conscious decision by both the member and the organization itself, while at the same time the integration of members into the organization no longer extended to the sum of their role relationships.

The process established itself slowly in such diverse areas as religion, business, and politics. As an example, beginning in the sixteenth century compulsory membership in a religious denomination became increasingly delegitimized. Prior to that, subjects were forced to share the religious denomination of their sovereigns. Consider the Anabaptist movement, which originated in Zürich. It called for a community of believers that was independent of the government and where members were not forced into a religion based on their birth, but were able to confess their faith freely as adults. A similar development took hold in the field of commerce. As the capitalist system evolved, the freedom of trade and economic pursuit established itself in a growing number of nations, thereby allowing citizens to engage in different kinds of work. The suspension of mandatory guild membership and the abolition of feudal subjection created the opportunity—and the necessity—for workers to offer their labor in the emerging "labor markets" (Marx, 1962: 183). In a largely parallel development, increasing opportunities arose to join special interest organizations, for instance, associations, political parties, or labor unions.

What are the special characteristics of organizations such as businesses, public administrations, universities, schools, churches, or the military? Which specific features make them different from spontaneous interactions in a supermarket, or from groups, families, or protest movements?

The Central Characteristics of Organizations

Without ever reading a single introduction or enrolling in a single course on organizations, we seem to know when we are dealing with one. We intuitively grasp that a draft notice from the military will result in contact with an organization. We realize that our support for our favorite team extends to the entire organization with all of its peculiarities; even occasional personnel changes do not put us off. And we are aware that by purchasing a bottle of olive oil, we are not entering into a contractual relationship with the cashier but rather with an organization that bears the name of the supermarket chain.

Even though we have this intuitive grasp, it is often difficult to define the special characteristics of organizations as compared to other entities like families, groups, protest movements, or an everyday conversation. Sociologist Niklas Luhmann—the leading system theorist and one of the most innovative organizational scientists of the twentieth century—uses three characteristics to illustrate the defining features of organizations in modern society, namely, membership, goals, and hierarchies.

Membership

As human rights have spread, the notion has arisen in modern society that all people have the right to be part of society by virtue of their birth. Even countries—which must not be equated with society—find it increasingly difficult to treat an individual as a non-person, as they would have a century or two ago. Admittedly, a state may refuse a person entry or a permanent residence permit, but there is a broad consensus that human rights must apply even to non-citizens. People continue to be denied their basic rights, so actual practice does repeatedly deviate from this standard. However, the media portray such events as scandalous, which indicates that they are understood as departures from prevailing norms (Luhmann, 1995: 16).

To a large degree, modern society has abandoned the practice of excluding its members. The death penalty, exile, and deprivation of citizenship are no longer part of the standard repertoire of measures countries take to ensure that their citizens conform to the rules. If misconduct occurs, the state may condemn, penalize, or imprison its citizens, but it cannot simply exclude them. If, in spite of this, a state resorts to standards well known from the Middle Ages, for example, death or exile for the purpose of doing away with an insurgent, it immediately exposes itself to the accusation of backwardness. One need only think of the vehement criticism of capital punishment as practiced in China, North Korea, or the USA, or the sharp condemnation of the deprivations of citizenship as conducted in the GDR, Iran, or Burma.

In contrast, one of the central characteristics of organizations is the decision regarding a person's entry or departure, in other words, the determination of membership (Luhmann, 1996b: 67). An organization, be it a business, a public administration, political party, or athletic club, can decide who is and who is not a member. And, of even greater consequence, it can determine who will cease to be a member because he or she is no longer following the rules. This allows organizations to stake out areas within which members (and only members) must submit to the rules. And the constant threat hangs in the air that members who break the rules will have to leave (Luhmann, 1964: 44f.).

Goals

Unlike societies in ancient or medieval times, contemporary societies overall refrain from adopting superordinate goals and from insisting that their citizens accept them. If attempts at defining such goals are to be found, for instance, in national constitutions—where they are limited to one country—they generally degenerate into very abstract expressions of values. To illustrate, according to the preamble of the American constitution, the objective is to "promote the general Welfare, and secure the Blessings of Liberty." In the case of the Constitution of the Russian Federation, the goal is "to ensure the well-being and prosperity" of the country and "assume responsibility for our Fatherland before the present and future generations." The propagation of very general values presumably does little harm, and politicians make ample use of them in their New Year's speeches. The matter becomes problematic, though, when a nation begins to make overly zealous commitments to a narrow goal program. We become wary when a country adopts goals like "achieving Marxist-

Leninist ideals for humanity," "proclaiming God's Word on earth," or "spreading capitalism across the globe," and then aggressively attempts to translate them into concrete programs which can be used to assess whether or not its citizens are living in accordance with these values (Luhmann, 1977: 39).

In organizations the situation is entirely different. Here, goals play a central role. Companies produce goods in the form of merchandise and services as a means of generating profit or—to cite an alternative goal—to meet the needs of the population. Authorities render public services and implement the framework that the political system has designated for society. The purpose of prisons is to hold convicts in custody and, in some countries at least, to rehabilitate them. Universities fulfill the twofold purpose of providing knowledge in specific fields of study to young adults, as well as conducting research. An organization that completely dispensed with formulating goals would create a tremendous amount of confusion both among its own members and in its external environment (Luhmann, 1973a: 87ff.). Even organizations whose goal is not readily apparent to outsiders at first glance—clubs, lodges, or student fraternities—attach great importance, at least in their external communications, to declaring goals like "furthering the community," "upholding moral standards," or "providing guidance and orientation for beginning students."

Hierarchy

Hierarchies are also losing importance in society (Luhmann, 1997: 834). Modern societies no longer have sovereigns who can extend their rule via chains of instructions or commands directly into various areas of the population's life. The determination of whether a theory can be accepted as scientifically valid is not made by a central agency that has the power to impose sanctions. The choice of who will govern a country is not made by an all-powerful institution, at least not in democracies. The question of which products to sell is not decided by a hierarchy, but results from market processes. The decision of whether something is beautiful or not doesn't fall under the authority of an omnipotent cultural appointee, nor do the workings of a hierarchy determine one's choice of a person to love.

As the examples of Iraq during the Saddam Hussein era or Afghanistan under the Taliban demonstrate, regimes that attempt to use hierarchical government structures to extend their rule into specific areas of the population's life are considered outdated and even potentially evil. The days are over when societies could organize themselves according to a strict hierarchy without encountering legitimacy problems. Today, there is no longer a king, emperor, or pope who can exert significant influence on the various areas of citizens' lives by activating his chains of command or instruction (Weber, 1976: 125). Nobody in our times would accept the president of the United States, the federal chancellor of Germany, or the president of the European Union Commission as a superior—with the sole exception of the staff at the White House, the chancellor's office, or the European Commission.

Unlike modern societies, organizations *are* hierarchically structured. Observers note that while large sections of society have been "de-hierarchicalized," scientific, political, artistic, and business organizations have retained their hierarchically structured systems. Immediately after seizing power and inspired by his dream of a society defined by hierarchy, Adolf Hitler referred to this difference in a speech before German generals. "Everybody knows," according to Hitler, "that democracy is out of the question in the military. It is also detrimental in the economic arena." The conclusion he draws seems abstruse from a contemporary perspective: given the dominance of hierarchies in businesses, the military, universities, and public administration, it was erroneous to conclude that democracy was possible in society. Therefore, society as a whole needed to be thoroughly and consistently structured according to the "Führer principle". Now that democracy has become the globally accepted norm, such attempts at "re-hierarchicalizing" can be viewed as failures for the most part. What we are hearing seems to reflect something else. Complaints are being voiced that democracy has been split, and the continued prevalence of hierarchies in businesses, public administration, hospitals, universities, and schools is viewed as a reason to call for the democratization of such organizations.

These attempts find surprisingly little support, however. Even for staunch advocates of democracy, the fun seems to end with the question of the internal structure of government agencies, companies, churches and universities. Businesses may debate whether their employees should have a greater say in company affairs, but a CEO who characterized her company as a democratic structure would presumably only make herself look ridiculous in the eyes of "her" employees. A governmental agency may debate whether it can dispense with managers at the department level, but there is no question that de-hierarchicalizing the agency itself would be labeled an infraction against a system that is anchored in constitutional law.

Decision-Making Autonomy

The ability of organizations to reach their own decisions about their goals, hierarchies, and membership is of central importance. We can only speak of an organization as a social system when a business, public administration, university, or hospital has the power to make its own independent decisions concerning who will or will not become a member. If the criteria for membership were imposed from without, it would restrict the organization's ability to place expectations on members and likewise to use the threat of dismissal to impose them. One need only think of developing countries where government agencies cannot recruit members independently, are permitted to hire personnel exclusively from a certain caste or designated clan, and also cannot dismiss employees when they are dissatisfied with them.

Decision-making autonomy becomes particularly clear in hierarchies. During the Middle Ages, it was still widely customary for the hierarchy of, say, a court, an army, or an agricultural production unit to reflect the hierarchy of the corresponding society as a whole. It was virtually unimaginable for a feudal lord to participate in a war as a simple soldier, while a serf assumed the role of commander. In modern societies, the tight linkage between class status and one's hierarchical rank within organizations has dissolved. Today, it is difficult to see internal organizational hierarchies—as can still be read in the works of Marx—as a simultaneous expression of class relationships in a society based on the difference between capital and labor. One's chances of becoming chairman of a corporation or the leader of a political party may still be greater now, as then, if one's father or mother previously held the position. Nevertheless, as a general rule it is an organization's own decisions that ultimately determine how positions within the hierarchy are filled.

Similarly, an organization's ability to define its goals autonomously is of pivotal importance. If goals are determined externally, and the organization cannot make such decisions independently, it limits the organization's opportunities to cultivate an identity of its own. It is then perceived as a mere lackey of some other, mightier entity. It becomes almost impossible to avoid the impression of being nothing more than a division of the larger organization. When reference is made to the liberation of businesses from centralized production planning, or schools shifting in the direction of independence, or the autonomy of universities based on academic freedom, it always also highlights the organizations' ability to determine their goal orientations independently.

Organizations are, of course, never completely independent in their decision making. After all, they are part of the society with its legal norms, political restrictions, and economic limitations. In the Western world at least, a company cannot decide to prioritize the hiring of workers in the eight-to-twelve-year-old range simply for reasons of efficiency. In the wake of an election, government agencies must expect that top positions will not be filled based solely on professional qualifications, but that membership in a particular party will figure prominently in the process. A company may decide to switch from offering security services to operating a protection racket, but it must then take into consideration that law enforcement authorities will not accept the goal change as if it were nothing unusual. In any event, the key issue is that within the limitations imposed by law, the political requirements, or economic shortages, organizations can make their own arrangements, which is to say, reach their own decisions, with respect to their goals, hierarchies, and membership.

CHAPTER 2

MEMBERSHIP, GOALS, AND HIERARCHIES

When one asks the members of organizations how their companies, universities, churches, political parties, or public administrations function, the descriptions received are often surprisingly simple. One need only look at the PowerPoint presentations that the employees of insurance companies use to depict the goals or the structure of their organizations, or the brochures that government agencies distribute at career fairs to recruit the next generation of administrators, or the websites that Greenpeace, the World Wildlife Federation, or labor unions use to attract members. The organizations always appear to have adopted a clear set of goals which are meant to be pursued through as efficient a form of organization possible (generally structured along hierarchical lines) and, of course, implemented by a well-trained staff.

A Simple Picture: From Goals to Hierarchies to Members

Even though the PowerPoint presentations, recruitment brochures, and websites don't always make it immediately apparent, in the final analysis the public face of an organization and the three organizational "ingredients" it displays, namely, goals, hierarchies, and membership, always paint a relatively simple picture of the organization as a goal-oriented structure. Organizations take an ultimate goal—such as producing automobiles, educating students, torturing regime critics, or providing pastoral care for the terminally ill—and break it down into subgoals and sub-subgoals. A specific division, department, or team within the organizational hierarchy is then assigned the responsibility of accomplishing each of these ends, and suitable members are recruited to fill the positions that have thereby been created.

In the Beginning Was the Goal

In the beginning, the goal is always foremost. After all, so the opinion runs, in its most basic form, the goal is ultimately the reason that the organization exists. Everything that transpires in the organization must be understood in terms of the primary goal which, in the final analysis, serves as the standard for all organizational activity. No matter what the purpose of the organization—manufacturing energy-saving lighting, designing web pages for craftsmen, chasing criminals, staging revolutions on Caribbean islands, or preventing the construction of nuclear power plants—according to this viewpoint an organization justifies its existence by achieving its goals.

Goal setting as the starting point has been presented to us in the traditional descriptions of organizations by economic, sociological, and psychological organizational research, where organizations are generally defined with reference to their goals and the means calculated for achieving them. As an example, an organization is then understood as a systematic, coordinated collaboration between individuals to create a product. Or, an organization may be defined as structures that pursue a goal over the long term and focus the activities of their members on accomplishing it.

According to the customary understanding of organizations, goals can be broken down into a large number of subordinate subgoals. Economist Adam Smith illustrated this idea with his famous example of the pin factory. Whereas a single uneducated worker would presumably not be able to produce even twenty push pins a day, Smith observed that splitting the goal of push pin production into a large number of subgoals would increase production enormously. The formation of subtasks such as drawing out the wire, cutting it, grinding the top, and attaching the pinhead, would allow each person to specialize in one task, thereby enabling ten people to produce a total of 48,000 pins per day (see Smith, 1999: 11).

Thus, it becomes possible to form complex means-end chains in organizations, whereby every end serves only as a means to achieve the end beyond, which, in turn, is only one link in a chain of further ends. According to an example given by organizational scientist and Nobel prize laureate Herbert Simon, a surprise attack on the front serves the purpose of capturing an enemy position; capturing the position, in turn, serves the purpose of breaking through the enemy front; breaking through the enemy front serves the purpose of forcing the enemy to capitulate; the enemy's capitulation serves the purpose of sealing victory with a peace treaty; and victory serves the purpose of strengthening the power of the country for which one has fought (Simon, 1957: 45ff.).

From this perspective, the organization appears to be a mere "organon," a tool or instrument with which the ever-present goal can be reached. It functions as an "organ" that has the ability to transform inputs in the form of raw materials, machines, or labor into desired outputs in the form of products, services, healed patients or educated students.

Responsibility Within the Hierarchy

According to this simple understanding of organizations, every goal, every subgoal, and every sub-subgoal can now be correlated with a position in the hierarchy. Ultimately, the means-end structure parallels the hierarchical structure (see Weber, 1976: 125). The leadership defines the way the organization wants to accomplish its goal. The actions required as means to achieve the goals are then "assigned to subordinates as tasks." These individuals "in turn, delegate subtasks to levels below them," until the "bottom of the hierarchy" is reached, which Luhmann calls the task performance level (Luhmann, 1971a: 96f.). Ultimately, the hierarchical order of positions is only a reflection of "the ordering of organizational ends and means" (see Luhmann, 1973a: 73).

Connecting the means-end relationship in parallel with the hierarchical differentiation between upper and lower, allows clear organizational analyses to emerge. Let's assume that the management of a company decides to become the global market leader in drill bit cassettes, those containers that allow us to arrange the bits neatly by size. Since the company's CEO bears final responsibility for achieving the goal of becoming world market leader, his next step is to determine which means are best suited to achieve his primary goal and who will be held accountable for achieving it. For example, he might determine that to become global market leader the company must conquer the Asian market. He would therefore appoint a director of sales who has responsibility for achieving that particular goal. She, in turn, will define subgoals for her subordinates, and in this fashion a position within the hierarchical structure is defined for even the smallest of goals.

Selecting the Right Members

If every position in the hierarchy is responsible for a certain range of tasks, then, according to this relatively simple understanding of organizations, all that remains is to fill the respective positions with suitable personnel. As early as the beginning of the twentieth century, rationalization expert Frederick Taylor was repeating the mantra, "choose the person who's best suited for the job" (Taylor, 1979: 44; see Morgan, 1986: 23). Almost contemporaneously, Max Weber (1976: 126) formulated the same thought when he observed that every task must always be performed by "a person with demonstrably successful professional training" if justice is to be done to the demands placed on a rational organization.

According to this understanding of organizations, it is always important to define the task first; then, as a second step, select the person with the exact qualifications to perform it. Business economists speak of the *ad rem* principle. Thus, tailoring a position to a person who has already been hired—the so-called *ad personam* principle—can only be understood as a pathology which is imaginable in exceptional cases at best. The selection of individuals, the logic runs, should always be geared to the tasks, and not vice versa, where the selection of tasks is geared to the individual (see Luhmann, 1971c: 209).

The first step, according to this line of reasoning, is to conduct a painstaking analysis of the task, thereby clarifying what needs to be done (the characteristics of the task to be performed), what needs to be acted upon (the object that needs to be changed), what will be used to perform the job (the available resources), where the task is to be performed (the workplace), and when it is to be performed (the time available). Following that, the analysis of the task determines how it is to be performed (the definition of the procedure). It is only after the task has been outlined in this manner that the qualifications are determined that will be required of the member who performs it.

Personnel selection, in this view, should be made solely and exclusively according to the criteria that are important for the organization. Factors such as ethnic origin, social background, gender, or sexual orientation are not supposed to play a role—or play a role only if they can be proven to work in the organization's interest. Research repeatedly shows that top economic positions are disproportionately held by individuals from upper-class backgrounds. This can be explained by the fact that members of upper-class cliques pull strings to obtain jobs for one another, which poses a problem for the organization's effectiveness. Or, in terms of rational personnel selection, the reason might be that socialization in upper-level families is free of the pressure to conform which otherwise prevails in organizations, and thereby promotes a change-oriented decision-making style that is particularly in demand in top-level positions. In contrast, it has been observed that for middle management positions the quality of stress resistance is particularly desirable; at that level managers are sandwiched between the very top and the very bottom and must reconcile a highly diverse range of demands and expectations. Meanwhile, at the very bottom of the organization an entirely different set of skills is in demand, for example, the willingness to perform mindless tasks without grumbling. It has been rumored that for this reason US corporations—in keeping with Frederick Taylor—conducted intelligence tests as part of the personnel selection process for "simple laborers." The object was not to recruit those with the most potential, but rather those whose intelligence was so low that they would not someday become dissatisfied with menial work.

Naturally, the question of who is the right person for the job can be contentious. Are people from higher social strata genuinely better suited for top business positions? Is the ability to bear up under stress truly a key qualification for middle managers? Might it be to the organization's advantage if even the people holding jobs at the very bottom weren't completely dense? In all of the controversies—at least according to this view—there is agreement that a scientifically based selection process will deliver the right people.

The Attractiveness and Limitations of a Purposive-Rational Understanding of Organizations

In organizational research, this perspective is adorned with complicated sounding scholarly terminology such as the "purposive-rational model" (see Weber, 1976: 12f.); the "rational perspective" (see Gouldner, 1959); or a "mechanical system" (see Burns and Stalker, 1961). The appeal of the position is obvious. Once the goal has been determined, this criterion can then be used to analyze the entire organization.

Naturally, an orientation based on an overriding goal includes heated discussions about which kind of corporate chart is best suited for the purpose and which type of personnel should be hired. Yet these discussions can always be conducted with relation to the overriding goal. If it happens that market assessments turn out to be incorrect, parts suppliers fall through, or individual employees refuse to perform, it can simply be recorded as a "deviation" from the organization's goal without preventing one from pursuing the goal in question.

Managers, Consultants and Researchers Share the Same Perspective

The charm of this model can be seen in the fact that the view of organizations held by managers, consultants, and researchers do not have to differ in principle. Management can make reference to the purpose of the organization as a way of justifying its ideas on optimization. If there are organizational units that cannot show very clearly what they contribute to achieving the ultimate goal—get rid of them. If the activities of staff members cannot be construed as a means of achieving the ultimate goal—rationalize them out of existence. Here, the difference in the position taken by labor representatives expresses itself only in the fact that they define "ultimate goal" in different terms, namely, to secure a livelihood for the employees, and consequently arrive at results that differ from those of management when it comes to breaking down operations into subgoals.

Consultants can simply adopt this purposive-rational perspective. Their task then consists of compiling the most complete body of information possible and, after carefully weighing the alternatives, suggesting to management or labor representatives more suitable means for achieving the ultimate goal. To this end, they dig deep into their toolboxes: business process reengineering, portfolio management, zero-based budgeting, time-based competition, the shareholder value concept or kaizen. It makes no difference which new-fangled method is propagated; the object is always to suggest a better way of achieving the goal.

When researchers adopt this purposive-rational perspective, as a rule they have no communication problems with adherents of the perspective in actual practice. Greatly simplified, disciplines such as business administration, pedagogy, and public health, which are closely geared to organizational practice, often view it as one of their central tasks to support companies, government agencies, or hospitals in achieving their goals through a scientifically based search for the proper means. It is considered self-evident to assume that the resource-intensive insights that have been gained for the organizations are at the same time also good science, or at least could be.

The Alternative: Describing Organizations "the Way They Are"

Unfortunately, however, it's not always that easy. The experiences of not only organizational scientists but particularly also of practitioners show that reality has little to do with this simplified purposive-rational understanding of organizations. The examples of the German-French technology concern Airbus, and US steel corporations illustrate that it is characteristic for some of the most long-lived organizations *not* to understand their own goals clearly, and that the work done by their mid-level managers does not qualify as particularly efficient and effective. Frequently, organizations do not form hierarchies to correspond with a goal, but rather because goals are being sought to correspond with already existing communication and decision channels. In addition to that, one occasionally has the impression that organizations are not looking for suitable personnel to fill precisely defined positions, but are creating positions for existing personnel instead. Life in organizations appears to be much wilder than the purposive-rational view would suggest.

Rather than simply labeling deviations from the purposive-rational model as pathology and viewing them as justification for ever-repeated attempts at optimization, a descriptive approach has established itself in organizational research. Organizations are described in a way that reflects how they really operate and not what they ought to be according to the dreams of a purposive-rational orientation. It is only in this fashion—based solely on the three central characteristics of goals, hierarchies, and membership—that a complex but realistic picture can emerge of the way organizations function, how they are structured, and how one can move within them as a member.

MEMBERSHIPS: THE MAGICAL MEANS TO CREATE ORGANIZATIONAL CONFORMITY

The first time a child observes its mother or father at the workplace can be a far-reaching experience. Somehow its parents seem to behave very differently at work and at home. Mother, who is caring and loving at home with the family, is an austere regent at "her" company. Father, who plays such an authoritarian role at home, quickly becomes subordinate the minute his manager enters the room. The child arduously learns that his parents act in peculiar, unaccustomed ways as soon as they are involved with an organization.

Organizations appear to produce unaccustomed behavior in their members, and to make them tolerate it as well. To quote Russian revolutionary leader Vladimir Ilyich Lenin: "Yes, this is indeed organization—when millions of men alter every aspect of their everyday habits, in new locations, in the name of a definitive goal, inspired by a definite will. In such a pursuit they adapt their methods of procedure, their armaments, and their tools to any change of circumstances and requirements."

Even if Lenin was thinking primarily of armies that are held together by force, or of revolutionary organizations which are characterized by a high degree of goal identification, in principle he might have been able to develop a similar sense of euphoria facing the harmonious, goal-oriented efforts of employees in major corporations, public administration, or universities.

In one branch of organizational science which draws on French philosopher Michel Foucault, the "funny behavior" seen in members of organizations prompts suspicions of subtle control strategies. The assumption is that the systems of rules inherent in daily activities, practices, and discourse exert power. With respect to the conduct of the members, the suspicion is that they can't really want to be behaving as they are right now. How can it be that people in organizations harmoniously fall into line and frequently act in ways significantly different from what their fellow human beings have otherwise come to expect?

The Clue: Conformity Is Created by Making Membership Conditional

To make people behave in unusual ways—at least from the perspective of observers who know them from other roles—organizations use a simple mechanism. They impose the condition that their members *must* fulfill such unusual behavioral expectations, at least if they want to become or remain members of the organization, "To begin with, only those who acknowledge the rules of the organization can join. And those who no longer wish to adhere to them must leave" (Luhmann, 2005b: 50; see also Luhmann, 1982b: 75 and Luhmann, 1996a: 345). It would obviously not go over well during a hiring interview, if one announced that one agreed with the organization's underlying orientation but was not willing to accept all of its rules.

The submission of members to the organization's expressed terms of membership has been described as adaptation to the organization's formal expectations. Such conditions of membership can be communicated in writing through a job description, work instructions, or an order to report for military service. Sometimes members are also required to provide written confirmation acknowledging an order, a new regulation, or new reporting relationship; this underscores the fact that the matter involves a condition of membership. Still, formalized expectations are frequently only communicated orally by a designee of the organization, for example, a manager. Regardless of the form chosen, it is important that the member realizes which expectations must be fulfilled in order to retain membership, and that everyone else can also rely on the individual having understood.

The Effect: Conformity is Produced

The only reason that organizations can achieve such a high degree of compliance in their members is because they are able to subject membership itself to a set of terms. The organization simply declares everything it considers good and important to be a mandatory obligation of membership. If a professional army needs its soldiers to be ready to secure elections in the Congo—and accept a six-month separation from their loved ones as a consequence—it can, on short notice, elevate a willingness to participate in the mission to the status of a formal expectation. The soldiers must either participate or resign from the organization.

The only explanation for the remarkable success organizations achieve in producing at least superficial conformity of action lies in this ability to make membership contingent on an array of conditions. Individuals who are "sluggish" and "stubborn," or who might have a tendency to be moody, are "domesticated" through the threat of having their membership terminated. It goes without saying that griping about executive incompetence is never-ending and that the latest management decision will be criticized or even covertly sabotaged, but open rebellion is extremely rare. Grumbling and complaining can be heard, but ultimately the formulated conditions of membership are fulfilled.

The conformity effect seen in organizations emerges quite clearly when they are compared to other social constructs that are not in a position to subject membership to the same kind of decision process. For example, in families, relationships between neighbors, or interactions within a circle of friends it is impossible to produce similar forms of congruity. When a mother forbids her child to smear the kitchen wall with crayons, and the child reacts with a defiant "Who cares!" and disobeys her, one can't simply terminate its membership in the family. The inability to terminate membership in a family can lead to a type of physical violence which does not normally arise in public administration, corporations, churches and universities.

Raising the Membership Question

The special thing about the expectations of membership is that they are violated when a member welches on so much as a single demand. The person who "rejects *one* of his superior's instructions" or "refuses on principle to recognize *one* of the regulations," is rebelling against "*all* of the organization's formal expectations," according to Luhmann (1964: 63). If an employee in the department of education outright refuses to comply with his supervisor's request to provide the file on a particular student, it will create significant organizational commotion. Yet the reason is not because that specific file is indispensable to the operation of the department of education, but rather because his non-compliance with even this small request must be interpreted as rebellion against the entire department's formalized expectations. If the captain of a national sports team were to criticize the coach's hiring decisions as "dishonest" and "disrespectful," he may be justified in doing so. Nevertheless, the organization cannot brook such criticism because it undermines the authority of the coach, and thereby ultimately the entire decision structure. Thus, such rebellion against authority will only be tolerated if the captain apologizes for his remarks to the coach personally as well as in public, and thereby acknowledges the terms of membership.

It is only because the central rules of membership focus on as much as a *single* explicit violation of the rules that organizations can establish formalized, across-the-board behavioral expectations in a way that is found virtually nowhere else in modern society. A member's every communication in the organization is accompanied in the background by the question of whether she is complying with formal expectations at that moment, and whether or not the rejection of a formal expectation will put her membership at risk. Particularly when problematical demands are made, the question that hangs in the air is: "Will I be able to remain a member if I openly reject such and such a demand as unreasonable?" (see Luhmann, 1964: 40).

The "Underlife"

Naturally, there are many different kinds of deviations from an organization's formal expectations. Life in organizations is much wilder than their written regulations and the orally communicated directives of superiors would suggest. Organizations have a significant underlife that is not taken into account if one examines only the formalized expectations on members.

Even so, we must make no mistake: behavior in organizations orients itself on the formal expectations. At a minimum, the formal expectations are always held available in reserve. They can be cited should the need arise, for example, when a subordinate—or a superior, for that matter—makes exaggerated demands. Or one can retreat to them if one wants to stay on the safe side (see Luhmann, 2005b: 60).

Membership Can Be Made Contingent on a Multitude of Conditions

Becoming a member of an organization entails accepting a multitude of conditions. For example, the organization's *goals*, or at least one of its relevant subgoals, must be affirmed if one wishes to remain a member. There is no expectation that members make a hobby of building nuclear weapons, producing eyeglass cleaning cloths, or selling real estate funds. But if one joins an arms manufacturing firm, a chemical company, or a bank, those goals must be adopted as one's own, at least during working hours. The organization's *hierarchies* must also be accepted, as well as instructions from members of the organization who have been designated as immediately superior to oneself—regardless of whether one respects the manager as a human being or considers her instructions purposeful. What's more, if the goal is to remain a member, one must accept the organization's other *members*. In life outside the organization it might be possible to avoid those "little idiots" to a large degree, but not so inside the organization, where collaborating with them numbers among the terms of membership.

Zones of Indifference

Much of what a member must accomplish cannot be precisely determined before joining the organization. It is impossible to communicate beforehand exactly which tasks the employees of a hospital, school, or corporation will confront. Granted, one can convey a basic sense of the goals the organization strives to fulfill and the activities that need to be performed to accomplish them. But it is extremely difficult to define in advance exactly how those factors will play out in terms of an individual employee's work package. While it is true that one can tell prospective members during a job interview where they will rank in the hierarchy, every member has to accept that their exact position will remain subject to determination by the organization. As well, one's future colleagues, the members of the organization with whom one will have to collaborate, can only be sketched out in broad strokes.

Herein lies the difference between a contract for services and a contract of employment. Organizations use a contract for services to purchase a precisely specified type of labor. Such contracts stipulate exactly which task is to be performed by when, and for whom. An employment contract, meanwhile, only allows organizations to acquire their members' time in a very abstract form. By signing an employment contract, members issue a kind of carte blanche and declare their willingness to put their abilities, creativity, and productivity to use in accordance with the tasks they are assigned. They forgo having the details of their job duties spelled out in written form (Commons, 1924: 284). Chester Barnard refers to such areas as "zones of indifference." Even though the areas are not defined in advance, members will be expected to comply, in other words, they must be indifferent about these zones of the organization (Barnard, 1938: 168ff.).

The Limits of Expectations on Members

Many of an organization's expectations clearly fall into the zone of indifference which members must accept. Police officers must reckon with chasing criminals; student assistants with having to copy books; and professors with the fact that they must instruct students in their field. Yet a number of expectations plainly fall outside of the zone of indifference that members can expect. Student assistants may assume that they will not be assigned to wash their professor's car. Professors must expect that although they will also have to instruct unmotivated university students, they will not be required to teach motivated elementary school pupils, say, in the event that their university courses are under-enrolled.

To gain an understanding of organizations, it is interesting to examine the border areas where it is unclear whether members must accept behavioral expectations or not. Is it permissible to expect student assistants to sort the books in their professor's private library? Can professors be expected to provide instruction in topics that do not fall within their field of expertise?

The Functionality of Generalized Membership Expectations

For organizations, having a zone of indifference that is as large as possible serves an obvious purpose. Members pledge a kind of limited, general obedience to instructions that are initially not specified in greater detail. Within such zones of indifference, organizations can adjust the expectations they place on their members without laborious internal negotiation processes. To put it concisely, a willingness to adjust to changes in the organization becomes a condition of membership itself (see Luhmann, 1991: 202).

In this manner, corporations, government agencies, or hospitals can modify their *goals* without having to seek prior approval from their members. They may also expect that members react with indifference to their classification in the *hierarchy*. Even if a member is getting along well with his current manager, he may be expected to accept a new manager even if she is younger than he, stems from a different milieu, or has been a member of the firm for a shorter period than he. And organizations may expect that changes in the composition of the *membership* will generally also fall into the zone of indifference. There is no need to obtain the approval of the entire staff every time a new member is brought on board.

Writer Jorge Semprún was active in the underground for the Communist Party of Spain during the Franco era and lived in constant danger of being arrested and tortured by the security police. He reports that after the Franco regime fell, it was the same individual members of the security police who had to accept the new hierarchy with himself in the position of minister. He describes how a police officer approached him during a state function and said, "Excellency, I was one of those who hunted you back then." During this dialogue, neither Jorge Semprún nor the police officer had any doubt that in order to remain on the police force the officer had to accept the change in the membership (the integration of former opponents of the regime into the organization), the hierarchy (former opponents of the regime had now even become his superiors), and of the goal (abandoning torture).

The zones of indifference represent a major advantage for organizations. Experience shows that members tolerate a high degree of change, disappointment, and stress within zones of indifference before they reach a decision to leave. The zone of indifference gives organizations the freedom to act according to their own judgment, thereby ensuring their existence through continual adaptation to a constantly changing environment (see Luhmann, 1964: 94).

How Do Organizations Motivate Their Members?

Organizations place far-reaching demands on their members. As an example, members might be expected to continuously turn screws in boreholes for eight hours, or drill in the barrack yard for four hours, or fold flyers and stuff them into business-sized envelopes. They are expected to dig up the streets with jackhammers when the temperature has reached ninety degrees in the shade, to shuffle files from one side of the office to the other, or to teach students who are exhausted from the heat or the overcrowded undergraduate classes.

How do organizations manage to make people submit to tasks that are not always so attractive? What are the mechanisms that make people remain members of an organization in spite of attractive alternatives such as spending time in a café, watching television, or having sex? What are the forces that bind people and make them actually fulfill an organization's expectations during the time it lays claim to them?

Money: The Charm of Material Incentives

When an observer thinks of ways to bond members to an organization, the first tool that comes to mind is money. If organizations are willing to pay accordingly, they can recruit members even for highly unattractive tasks such as cleaning oil-polluted beaches, photocopying thick books or processing building permits. And since people are in chronic need of money, members can be bound to a work organization not only over the limited term but permanently.

Generally speaking, the members of organizations are paid directly in the form of wages, a salary, or bonuses in return for making themselves available to work for part of the day. Yet there are still other variations where motivation is not created through direct payment from the organization, but merely through the prospect of receiving payment from others. Corporations have developed a personnel recruitment practice whereby interns do not need to be paid at all anymore and instead can be motivated simply by the prospect of receiving payment at a later time. Particularly in developing countries, government agencies can afford to pay their members very poorly or not at all, because the allure of working as a police officer, customs agent, or employment placement officer does not lie in the direct government salary, but in the opportunity to pocket bribes.

The advantage of using money to bind members lies in the flexibility of this medium. Monetary payment can induce members to accept a change from highly motivating goals (saving children with AIDS) to goals that are less so (selling AIDS medications for profit). Payment can induce them to tolerate demotivating information over an extended period of time, for example, as might pertain to the lethal side effects of newly developed pharmaceuticals. Further, it allows organizations to hire executives who may well distinguish themselves in terms of professional competence, but do not have a particularly motivating effect on their subordinates. Since the members' willingness to comply has been secured through monetary payments, the organization can do without charismatic leadership (Luhmann, 1964: 94ff.).

The disadvantage, however, is that organizations are dependent on constantly finding new sources of income to retain their members. Businesses accomplish this by selling the products their members produce and using the revenues to ensure that there is money to meet the payroll. Public administrations must rely on tax revenues to pay their agents and employees. Associations, NGOs, and political parties that do not rely exclusively on a volunteer workforce require a steady stream of membership dues, contributions, and government subsidies if they want to bring full-time professionals on to the staff as well.

Force: Using the Threat of Violence to Impose Expectations on Members

Force is a method of motivating people that proved effective in all of the advanced civilizations during antiquity, the Middle Ages, and the early Modern Age and continues to be used by some organizations to this day. The force exerted by the organization consists of permitting members to leave only under circumstances that have been defined by the organization. To this end, organizations institute their own means of coercion such as an internal policing agency (the military police, for example), their own judicial system (as in military tribunals), and their own prisons, all for the purpose of forcing participation in their activities. Or, they utilize governmental prosecuting authorities to ensure that members who escape are arrested, convicted, and imprisoned. The purpose of the coercion is to set exit costs so high that members generally do not view withdrawal as a serious option.

As a method of recruiting and retaining members, force has lost popularity in modern society although it is still applied in governmental organizations. Pertinent examples include the military, where both conscripts and professional soldiers are forbidden to quit under threat of imprisonment or even execution; militias, where members are permitted to lead "normal" lives—with the exception of occasional exercises—but are called up for mandatory service in the event of an emergency; police forces in times of war, when police officers are prohibited from resigning; border troops that do not offer their members the option of leaving the unit; companies that achieve their production goals through forced labor; and social welfare agencies that draw heavily on individuals who are performing their alternative national service and are therefore under obligation to work for them.

The advantage of motivating members by force is obvious. The organization can acquire a large number of members for frequently unattractive and dangerous tasks. Particularly in wartime, the tasks arising in the military, the police force, or militias are associated with grave hardship and risks, making it unlikely that sufficient volunteers could be found to perform them.

The disadvantage for organizations that coerce their members into service, however, is that it becomes difficult to achieve compliance that goes beyond the members' mere presence. In organizations where people become members of their own accord and are also free to leave again, the threat of termination or expulsion plays a central role in their compliance. But precisely this mechanism is not available in the same form to organizations that bind their members through force. Here, refusing to comply must not be allowed to become a question of dismissal, but must perforce become an issue involving the judicial system, either the organization's own or that of the state. Organizations must deploy enforcement staff to punish infractions and impose the expectations of the organization. Maintaining an enforcement apparatus not only consumes vast resources, but also frequently creates legitimation problems for such organizations.

Identifying with Organizational Goals

A further way to bind members to an organization is to offer them attractive goals. Rescuing neglected children, protecting the environment, providing assistance for impoverished countries in Africa, the global revolution, or the founding of a new nation are such appealing goals that they themselves can be enough to make people join.

As a rule of thumb, the more motivating the goals the lower the salaries. Political parties, hospitals, developmental aid organizations, or companies involved in green enterprises are therefore often in a position to offer their full-time professionals lower salaries than other organizations because such individuals identify so strongly with their goals. Many times the members are actually willing to pay for being allowed to join—in the form of membership dues.

Yet even when members do not join because they find the organization's goal particularly attractive, there is a prevailing hope in the organization that it can be made clear to them how attractive the goal really is. Chester Barnard observed that it is not enough to retain employees through wages, status symbols, or the prospect of a career (Barnard, 1938: 149ff.). Rather, the object is to influence the members' needs and utility functions in such a way that they feel as if their own interests coincide with those of the organization. "We have successfully positioned a new high-pressure cleaner in the market" or "When it comes to carbon dioxide separation and storage, we're great." When employees use sentences like that in their private conversations, it is an indication that efforts to foster employee identification with organizational goals are often successful. It reminds one of Max Weber's thoughts on the Protestant ethic which, in his opinion, ultimately leads to pursuing work activities as an ideology, an absolute end in itself (see Weber, 1965: 52).

Employee identification with an organization's goal is associated with the hope that they will perform better if a work process is stabilized through self-interest. The belief is that an organization functions better if identification with its approach has not been bought with high salaries and bonuses, lavish company cars with teak-trimmed interiors, or travel incentives promising celebrity vacations, but instead is viewed as part of the employees' personal interest. The operative assumption is that people are more motivated if they are fascinated by the cause itself and consequently can identify with the norms and values systems of the enterprise.

Nevertheless, identification with goals also has its disadvantages. It may sound surprising at first, but it causes organizations to sustain a considerable loss of flexibility. When employees identify with their goal, argues Niklas Luhmann, the organization loses elasticity (see Luhmann, 1964: 137ff.). The stonemason whose self-definition consisted of contributing to building a cathedral was probably difficult to employ in other medieval construction projects. An employee who derives his motivation primarily from providing a highly specific product to the customer will be difficult to enthuse about selling a different product. Another employee, who is responsible for flexibility in the handling of work packages within her group and identifies very strongly with her job, may encounter motivation problems if she is suddenly required to perform in a completely different area. The "tragedy" of the matter is that when a business makes an all-out effort to promote employee identification with a certain product or process, it limits its capacity to act in precisely that area. Wherever employee motivation is particularly strong, change becomes particularly difficult. For a company that relies on adjusting to constantly changing conditions in the marketplace and the environment, it would be especially onerous to expect that employees would identify personally with each set of circumstances the business encountered.

The Attractiveness of Activities

A further means of binding members to an organization consists of offering them attractive activities. Consider volunteer fire departments or disaster relief organizations such as the Red Cross or Red Crescent, which retain their members primarily by providing interesting work assignments. Or one need only think of the recreation trainers at vacation resorts who are primarily motivated by directing physical activities on the beach for which others are willing to pay.

A number of organizations bond with their members almost exclusively by offering them attractive activities. People become members of baseball clubs because they like to run after a ball, they join sailing clubs because they enjoy boating, and they join smoking clubs associated with restaurants so they can continue pursuing their addiction indoors. In these cases, the opportunity to participate in an activity is the members' specific reason for joining, and they are often prepared to pay.

Yet the highly attractive activities can go, but do not necessarily, hand-in-hand with the attractiveness of the organization's goals. In speaking with people who are involved with the church-based youth work, or caring for the handicapped, one learns that it is not only a case of viewing the goal as meaningful, but also the enjoyability of the activity itself. In comparison, the recreational trainers at a seaside resort, the graphic artists in advertising agencies, or the next generation of players in a major basketball league find a great deal of enjoyment in their activities, but they will find it relatively difficult to convey a high degree of identification with their organizations' goals to their circle of acquaintances.

From an organizational perspective, the attractiveness of activities offers advantages similar to those of identification with goals. If people take joy in an activity, it presents an opportunity to reduce their pay or even dispense with it altogether. Consider the many "dream jobs" such as commercial art, singing, or acting. They are attractive activities in an immediate sense, but for this very reason command relatively modest pay, at least in terms of averages. To a large extent, organizations can also do without monitoring members' concrete willingness to participate because the members themselves perceive their activities as attractive. Critics belittle attempts to make work assignments more attractive, referring to them as "cow sociology" or "cow psychology" because they are based on the assumption that happily grazing cows will produce better milk and also more of it.

Conversely, the disadvantages of this form of motivation are clear as well. Organizations that motivate members primarily through the attractiveness of their activities have very limited options. After all, they must ensure that all of the required activities have a high fun factor—or at least some of the activities should entail such a high fun factor that members are also willing to perform the less attractive, mandatory ones. Few organizations can offer exclusively attractive activities, however, so this factor generally plays only a supporting role in motivating the membership.

Collegiality

Yet another factor binding members to an organization can be seen in the collegiality that arises between them. Organizational research has repeatedly tried to prove that members are both more contented and more willing to perform when they form close ties to their colleagues. For instance, according to the assumptions of the so-called human relations approach, having colleagues satisfies the need for contact and fellowship with others.

During the Second World War, Edward A. Shils and Morris Janowitz (1948: 280ff.) conducted research on the far-reaching motivational effect of collegiality. Based on surveys of German soldiers, they arrived at the conclusion that combat motivation did not depend primarily on agreement with Nazi ideology (motivation through identification with goals), the joy of killing (motivation through attractive activities), access to larger salaries or looting opportunities (financial motivation), or fear of punishment at the hands of the National Socialist enforcement apparatus (motivation through force). Instead, it was based on a sense of duty toward a group of comrades. As these collegial relationships were torn apart through mounting casualties over the course of the war, signs of disintegration could be observed in the Wehrmacht in addition to a growing inclination to desert, and a concurrent rapid decline in bonding to the organization.

The advantage of motivation through collegiality is obvious. Particularly direct colleagues have a pronounced disciplining effect on members' behavior. The reason is that colleagues will intervene with advice, admonishment, and, as an ultimate consequence, sanctions if another member of the organization violates his duties. Since the imposition of norms established by colleagues tends to take place in the shadow of the formal order, it is not infrequently more effective— and often more brutal toward those affected—than an official threat of punishment or termination from a superior.

Nevertheless, collegiality-based norms can also turn against an organization, which is a disadvantage at least from an organizational perspective. Particularly the expectations of collegiality that arise in cliques, those informal coalitions of a small number of members, can have the effect that deviations from the forms of behavior expected by superiors become obligatory. According to Renate Mayntz (1963: 130), collegiality-based norms can "dampen the pace of work," "reward insubordination to superiors with recognition," and cover up lapses that are problematical for the organization.

As a rule, collegiality alone does not constitute sufficient motivation to join an organization. A corporation, public administration, or NGO will probably not succeed in attracting members if a pleasant working environment is its only recruitment tool and, other than that, it is not in a position to apply force, pay appropriate salaries, offer a truly attractive goal, or feature entertaining activities. All the same, collegiality can be very useful in reinforcing motivation in members who have joined for other reasons.

Dovetailing, Change, and Neutralization

The list of various forms of membership motivation can be used to distinguish different types of employees based on their predominant motivation. A number of such approaches have been undertaken, particularly in the field of psychology. This might involve differentiating between, say, employees who identify strongly with the goals of the organization—the "we-at-XYZ-corporation" type who are genuinely convinced that the dandruff shampoo "their firm" produces really is the best. Or, consider the "mercenaries," who are indeed high performers but are motivated solely by money and would switch to a better paying competitor without hesitation.

Distinctions between forms of motivation can also be used to classify organizations. For example, one speaks of *normative organizations*. People join such organizations to achieve their political, religious, or cultural ideals. Normative organizations are dominated by intense member identification with the organization's goals. *Utilitarian organizations* are those which motivate their members through salaries, bonuses, or other incentives. And *coercive organizations*, finally, are prepared to "motivate" their members through imprisonment, corporal punishment, or death (see Etzioni, 1961: 23ff.).

Nevertheless, attempts at identifying personnel and organizational types according to the five forms of membership motivation offer little satisfaction. They tend either to classify people in categories along the lines of "Which organizational type are you?" while overlooking that it is precisely the mixtures of membership motivations that are of interest. Or, they depict organizations almost as caricatures because they can only imagine one form of membership motivation per organization. The forms of motivation become interesting when they are used to define the combinations, shifts, and conflicts among motivational situations.

As a rule, organizations employ a combination of methods to motivate their members. Businesses that are forced to reward their members primarily in monetary form additionally attempt to promote the meaningfulness of their goals, even if it involves the production of sanitary napkins, chocolate spreads, or land mines. The military, which recruits its members through coercive mechanisms during wartime, can also attempt to convey the purposefulness of the war and offer monetary rewards beyond a salary, for example, at the cost of the conquered population. For organizations, the charm of strong identification with their goals is that they do not have to pay their members, but can instead, under certain circumstances, even receive payment from them. Often, however, it takes further incentives than goal identification to produce motivated commitment. As an illustration, an important inducement for making a commitment to a political party can lie in facilitated access for members to jobs that are financially lucrative as well.

What is more, the core motivational situation in an organization may shift. Many a political organization began as an initiative founded by unsalaried individuals who identified strongly with the goals, for example, protecting seal pups or preventing pharmaceutical exports to the Third World. At some point, the organization continues to exist only because its increased size and the chance to acquire government subsidies or private funding enable it to provide a livelihood for an ever-growing number of members, thereby (if for no other reason) damning the organization to permanence. Politically committed individuals, whose convictions were their initial reasons for joining an action group for development policy, a liberal or conservative political party, or a fascist splinter group, now realize that their involvement has led to an opportunity for a full-time or part-time professional occupation. By and by, economic motives persuade them to stay in the organization even though their identification with its goals has declined. Sports teams such as Manchester United in Great Britain initially motivated their members through the attractiveness of the activity, although with increasing professionalization they were forced to (and generally also in a position to) motivate their players with money. On the other hand, it can also happen that the initial reason for joining a team, in other words, the pleasure of playing the game, is overlaid with the motive of enjoying the fellowship of others who share one's love of the sport. The one-time enthusiastic soccer player winds up as a potbellied goalie whose main focus is "the third half-time" at the tavern.

The situation becomes particularly interesting when conflicts arise between members with respect to their motivation. The management of disaster relief organizations such as the Red Cross or the Salvation Army operates under the "self-evident" assumption that goal identification is the factor motivating the majority of their members to rescue the injured, see to their needs, and care for the latter if they have become disabled. Therefore, the managers offer at best to reimburse workers for their costs and are taken by surprise when emergency medical technicians and the staff of homeless shelters confront them with the fact that the organizations are not even paying minimum wages. In many political youth organizations, the lack of knowledge about the party platform among the party's own members indicates that the recruitment of the next generation is not being driven by identification with the party program but rather by the prospect of exciting fêtes, attractive sex partners, and fast-track careers. Because of the mixed motivational situation, those who are acting on conviction, those who are pursuing careers, and the "party animals" collide and must laboriously reach agreement on a mixed organizational orientation that is capable of integrating the different forms of membership motivation.

Aside from any heterogeneity of membership motivations, one point remains key: in their day-to-day operations, organizations are able to abstract from the motives of their individual members to a considerable extent (Luhmann, 1964: 42). Regardless of what induced a person to join a company, association, or political party—identification with its goals, the prospect of financial reward, or the positive mood among its members—the organization can expect that its members will abide by the rules for as long as they wish to remain affiliated with it (Luhmann, 2010: 200). Thus, all the discrepancies notwithstanding, an organization can reckon with "homogenous membership motivation." The burdensome necessity of examining the reasons why individuals actually became members arises only under exceptional circumstances such as employee crises, strategy conferences, or conflicts between management and employee representatives. As Niklas Luhmann succinctly remarked: "Soldiers march, clerks keep records, and ministers of state govern, whether it pleases them in a certain situation or not" (Luhmann, 1975b: 12).

Limitations of Membership

If one is to believe the often idealized descriptions of organizational life in the "good old days" after the Second World War, in those times the question of who was a member of which organization was far less ambiguous and subject to change than today. When people entered work life—at least so it would appear in retrospect—they would join an organization such as Ford, the postal service, or the municipal government and then stay there until their working lives came to an end. Since this generally entailed being tied to one location, they could also become lifelong members of the local sports club, the church choir, or the local chapter of a political party. As well, they remained loyal to the same political party for their entire lives, or so it would seem in romanticizing retrospectives.

Yet if we can believe the analyses stemming from the times themselves, such unequivocal definitions of memberships must be increasingly called into question.

The Fuzziness of Organizational Membership

As the number of "normal" employer-employee relationships, in other words, full-time employment for an unlimited period in the company, public administration, or hospital continues to dwindle, many researchers are finding that it is becoming increasingly difficult to arrive at a clear definition of an organization's circle of members. The so-called "atypical occupations," which are characterized by limited-term contracts, part-time employment, or a decoupling between the firm providing the employment and the de facto workplace, are increasingly turning into "typical occupations" in the brave new world of work. But there are indications that "normal membership conditions" are increasingly unwinding in political, labor, and cultural organizations as well. Instead of remaining a member of the Republican or Democratic Party for many years, people now participate in a particular campaign, become involved within the framework of a trial membership, or engage as active donors to a specific party initiative.

The field of labor leasing is an illustrative example of the growing difficulty one encounters in classifying membership. In temporary work or labor leasing, a leasing company hires employees for the long term and then leases them out for short-term assignments. By separating the employer-employee relationship (between the leased worker and the temporary employment agency) on the one hand, from the work relationship (with the organization that occupies the temporary workers) on the other, the user company gains flexibility and can acquire or unload personnel quickly. However, it becomes increasingly difficult to determine to which of the two entities the activities of the temporary workers can be attributed.

Contemporary analyses outline this development using terms such as an "intrapreneur" or a "Me Inc." According to this diagnosis, everybody markets his or her own "ego shares" and is responsible, as an independent brand leader, for the development of a product called "Me." People no longer view themselves as members of an organization—as an "organization man" or a "corporate man." Instead, they are increasingly engaging as "entrepreneurs within the enterprise."

According to this diagnosis, the development is increasingly leading to difficulties in defining who still belongs to an organization and who doesn't. Can the staff at the administration lounge still be counted as members of the organization when the canteen has been spun off as an independent service company which is fully owned by the administrators? Who is accountable for the mistakes made by someone who is employed by a temporary employment agency but has put in years with a single automobile manufacturer: the temp agency or the manufacturer? If a consultant who works on a fee basis operates within an organization for an extended period of time, does she then count as a member?

Organizational Boundaries Become Fluid

The difficulty of assigning people to organizations is aggravated by increasingly rapid cycles of spinning off widely diverse operations and subsequently at least partially reintegrating them. Internal functions such as security services, the canteen, or data processing are first outsourced to external service providers and suppliers, only to be reintegrated into the organization at a later time.

Outsourcing allows organizations to create market relationships in areas that previously involved internal negotiation processes between departments. The process is driven by the hope that competition between various providers will lower costs and raise quality. Yet when organizations realize that the cost savings are paltry, that their ability to exert control has decreased, and they have surrendered their core competencies, they are often moved to perform the services themselves in the future or to buy out the external service provider. Then the situation once again involves relations within the organization as opposed to relations between organizations.

As such, outsourcing and insourcing are not new phenomena. After all, even the decision to commission an external service provider such as the postal service with the delivery of a letter, rather than delivering it to the addressee oneself, represents a classical decision between "making" (delivering the letter oneself) or "buying" (purchasing delivery as a service). What appears to be new is the speed at which organizations are alternating between outsourcing and insourcing. For many businesses today, shifting back and forth between the two, that is, between buying goods or services from others and providing them oneself seems to have become business as usual.

An illustrative example of this back and forth can be observed in the logistics of automobile manufacturing. In earlier times, car companies themselves organized the flow of parts to their assembly lines. Then these logistical functions were outsourced to a large degree. Outside companies delivered the parts directly to the production lines, where they were installed by employees of the automobile manufacturing company, although partially also by subcontractors. But a number of the external suppliers were unable to adapt to the complexities of the production process, and as a result production-related logistics were reintegrated to some degree. Some automobile companies constructed new distribution centers so that they could take control of logistics themselves—which presumably will continue until outsourcing the logistic function is in favor once again.

Observation shows that rapid alternation between insourcing and outsourcing makes it increasingly difficult to determine whether the units that provide a service for an organization should be classified as internal departments or as external partners. How does one classify the employees who deliver parts to the production line every day on behalf of an outside company? If a group of data processing specialists have been officially spun off but continue to provide their services on location from their old offices, just as before, who do they identify with? What about employees who have been spun off and subsequently reintegrated into a company a number of times within an insourcing and outsourcing framework?

The Formation of Organizational Networks

When organizations are networked, it becomes even more difficult to define their boundaries in greater detail and thereby also to assign membership. In the economic arena, the term "network" refers to forms of collaboration on research and development, production, and sales that lie beyond the invisible hand of the market and the iron fist of a hierarchy. In politics, networks of organizations form, for example, when over a longer period of time various left-leaning organizations link up to combat rightist extremism, or right-leaning organizations become affiliated to combat leftist extremism. In science as well, forming networks between universities, research institutes, and businesses is par for the course, at least if one wishes to create the impression of excellence (see Bommes and Tacke, 2005: 282ff.).

In contrast to organizations, networks have poorly defined contours. This makes it difficult to determine who—in terms of the social dimension—is actually part of them. While collaboration within networks is frequently spelled out in the form of a contract, the network itself generally arises in a fluid fashion as ideas for projects develop, talks intensify, or collaboration begins to occur on a more regular basis. Repeated agreements, subcontracts, or project collaborations lead to the affiliation of further partner organizations. Meanwhile, other collaborators drop out of the network for an extended period of time—this often goes completely unnoticed by the others or even partners themselves—simply because they no longer participate in the same form as before, or because their attendance at meetings becomes irregular.

Networks are generally also not as easy to define as organizations in terms of the time dimension. Granted, cooperative endeavors within networks often have an "official" beginning when representatives from the various organizations gather for a kick-off conference, the signing of a contract, or a first joint appearance before the media. But by then, generally speaking, collaboration between the network partners has already begun in the form of exploratory talks or pilot projects, or on the basis of previous cooperative ventures. It is also typical that collaborations within networks are not formally terminated. Instead, they either run their course unnoticed or transition seamlessly to a new cooperative venture.

A final characteristic of networks is that there is often a lack of clarity about the factual dimension, which is to say, who performs which tasks. Since performance allocation often cannot be spelled out clearly in contractual form, and no hierarchical authority comes into play, many network partners have the impression that they are doing more than others. To quote an often-heard saying in these circles, a network is like a huge inflatable cushion: "everybody's trying to inflate it, and everybody thinks they're blowing harder than anybody else."

The more organizations form networks and the more cooperation within organizations is replaced by collaboration within the network, the more difficult it becomes to classify personnel. Do people feel a connection with the network or with the organization that dispatched them? How does one manage their affiliations when they are members of several different participating organizations, as is often the case? If people (and, going one step further, their performance) are so difficult to sort out in networks, then who "owns" the goods and services that a network produces? If such a high degree of indeterminacy prevails, how does one distribute the proceeds?

Conclusion: A Closer Look at Organizational Boundaries

In light of these developments, how important does the category of organizational membership remain? Is it still relevant in current sociological discussions of the "disintegration of the organization," the "dissolution of organizational boundaries," or "networks as structural forms beyond market and hierarchy?" Given the emergence of so-called "virtual networks" encompassing a large number of collaborating independent employees, is it even still possible to discuss membership as a central organizational criterion? Does the disappearance of the normal employer-employee relationship based on a Monday to Friday workweek from 8:00 AM to 4:00 PM also erode the role of membership?

Due to questions such as these, there is a tendency in organizational research to relativize the concept of membership and partially even to abandon it entirely. Organizations are then understood merely in terms of loose networks where people converge for highly specific projects. There are prognostications of "borderless organizations," and a rise in "virtual organizations" has been observed. Ultimately, it raises the question of whether organizations are "disintegrating" (see Ashkenas et al., 1998).

Nevertheless, the opposite would seem to make sense. The more the definition of membership is called into question, the more intensely all of those involved are examining just what constitutes an organization and what doesn't. Growing virtualization, permanent shifts in boundaries, and their erratic placement and removal appear to be causing boundaries to come under even closer scrutiny. If businesses continue to trend in the direction of employing temporary workers, then even more energy will be expended on defining where the temporary agency's responsibilities end and where the user company's begin. If universities switch over to handling teaching assignments through short-term contracts or through adjuncts working under highly specific service contracts, those in charge of such matters will increasingly begin to wonder which of the adjuncts' rights and obligations qualify them for the same treatment that "regular" university employees receive, and which do not.

Organizations cannot dispense with monitoring people's activity from the membership standpoint. Even if corporations, public administrations, universities, and churches are constantly refining the concepts of "internal" and "external," and even if there may be individuals who are ambivalently positioned, that doesn't mean that membership as a category loses its value as an orientation point. Therefore, managing memberships and deciding where to draw the limits of membership require all the more attention and take on even greater importance as a cardinal means of shaping organizations.

GOALS: THE ORGANIZATIONAL ROLE OF PURPOSES

Organizations are imaginative in formulating their goals. "We will increase our market share in South America from 7 to 8.5 percent." "Next year we will reduce discards by ten thousand parts per year" or "Our management ensures that all our employees are contented, and as a result we never lose more than one employee per month." Such are the goal statements that can be found in businesses, whereas in labor unions we find goal statements along the lines of "We will gain 800 new members in three months" or "The strike on the West Coast will produce wage increases of at least 4.5 percent."

When businesses, public administrations, hospitals, or branches of the military set out in search of their long-term goals, they like to refer to the process as goal identification or strategy development. Often, top management's main task is seen as preparing the organization for a change in goals by developing a strategic vision (see Chandler, 1962: 15). Consulting firms focus on strategy processes in which they critically examine the goal orientation of the organizations that have commissioned them and suggest alternative orientations if necessary.

Which functions do purposes, goals or—as one might say using management jargon—strategies fulfill?

Organizational "Blinders"

A small thought experiment will illustrate the function of goals. In principle, an organization has free choice in deciding on a goal. It might provide free medication for children in the Third World and solicit donations from the public to that end. Yet it could also increase its own profitability by selling expensive but ineffective vitamin drinks to concerned parents. Instead of selling medicinal vitamin cocktails for children, it might sell milk drinks—perhaps the profit margins would be even greater. Or it could use the sale of vitamin cocktails for children merely as a vehicle to disseminate information on healthy nutrition during early childhood. A further option might be to adopt the view that children are entirely irrelevant and decide to advocate on behalf of independent window cleaners, reconstruct the history of a city neighborhood, or prepare for the next mission to the moon. In terms of selecting a potential focus, organizations find themselves, at least theoretically, in a realm of unlimited possibilities.

But even if the resources and the will to achieve all of these goals existed simultaneously, the organizations are forced to concentrate on only one or two of the many options. No later than the point when debate arises over which goal should be favored in the event that objectives clash, or which goals deserve to receive particularly large allocations of resources, the organization itself will begin to narrow the range of its choices. One refers to such determinations undertaken within a theoretically unlimited array of possibilities as *goal setting*.

Setting One Goal Always Implies Forgoing Another

Setting goals always implies a dramatic narrowing of an organization's horizon. Goals focus attention on a handful of possible aspects that appear to be key, while screening out everything else. Goal setting emphasizes the commanding importance of one particular aspect but always at the cost of ignoring, if not actually damaging, a large number of other potential angles.

In that sense, one can refer to strategies or goals as an organization's "blinders" (see Luhmann, 1973a: 46). Just as horses have a very wide field of vision due to the lateral placement of their eyes, organizations also have the option, at least in principle, of expanding their horizons almost as far as they wish. And much the way blinders prevent horses being distracted from behind or the side, goal setting prevents organizations from becoming confused by a plethora of other possibilities.

The setting of goals—the blinders—produces a highly simplified view of the organization's environment (see Luhmann, 1973a: 192). If a company's goal is to become the market leader in hard drives, then it needn't think about alternative markets such as display screens or CPUs. If the purpose of the army is to protect the population of its own country from attacks by neighboring states, then the military command doesn't need to occupy itself with alternative goals such as quashing revolts in the interior or preparing for military interventions in other countries.

Goals Mobilize the Choice of Means

The narrower horizon brought about by goal setting fulfills yet another important function. It focuses the organization's strength on reaching the goal and mobilizes thinking about the means best suited for accomplishing the task. If a company's goal is to number among the world's top three in the field of agricultural utility vehicles, it will compare itself with other companies in the industry and use a so-called benchmarking process to determine whether there might not be other, even better suited ways of producing tractors.

In search logic the saying holds that "The end justifies the means" (see Luhmann, 1973a: 46). After all, the function of goals is to mobilize as much creative thinking as possible in the choice of appropriate means. Generally, however, the choice of means which may be applied is always restricted. If the management of a hydroelectric power plant producer announces that it has the goal of conquering the Greek and Turkish markets, then it is at least questionable whether bribery would be a legitimate means of achieving that end.

Taking a look at the means that an organization considers acceptable for achieving a goal tells us a lot about it. Do a country's security forces respect the prohibition of torture, or does the alleged or actual threat of terror make them so desperate that they will resort to almost any means? Is the development of a new cancer medication so crucial to the survival of a pharmaceutical manufacturer that it issues a directive to develop a suitable drug regardless of cost, or does it issue clear instructions setting maximum cost limits?

In organizational science, the search for the optimal means to achieve a goal is called *purposive rationality*. This rationality does *not* refer to the choice of the goal. The goal has already been set. Rather, it is a question of searching for the appropriate means to accomplish the purpose. The goals themselves may appear highly dubious to observers—constructing internment camps for political dissidents, training suicide attackers, or manufacturing hairspray. Nevertheless, one would credit the organization with a high degree of purposive rationality if it chose the means to achieve its goal as effectively and efficiently as possible. As prominently formulated by sociologist Max Weber, acting in a purposive-rational manner initially entails weighing different goals against one another, giving consideration to possible adverse side effects, and then selecting the most appropriate means to achieve the defined ends (see Weber, 1976: 13).

The Difficulty with Goals

There are a good number of organizational scientists who view goals as so important that in their opinion organizations are nothing other than the means to achieve an end. To illustrate, philosopher and sociologist Theodor Adorno (1990: 441) characterized organizations as deliberately established and managed purposive associations. Sociologists Peter M. Blau and Richard W. Scott (1962: 5) identified the characteristic feature of organizations as the fact that they have been expressly created for the purpose of achieving certain goals. And sociologist Amitai Etzioni (1964: 3) subsequently defined organizations in even more direct terms as social units created to "pursue specific goals."

Unfortunately, it's not that simple. While it is true that goals exert a significant structuring effect, they frequently play a much more complicated role than purpose-oriented definitions of organizations would suggest.

Conflicting Purposes

Organizations often endorse a whole array of goals, thereby implying that the ends are compatible with or even support one another. The presidents of universities simultaneously propagate excellence in research, an exquisite scientific education for a large numbers of students and highly targeted preparation for professional life— suggesting that all three goals can be optimally achieved at the same time. In practice, however, organizational goals often clash.

As an example, some companies define their goals in terms of having profitable business operations, tapping new markets, developing fundamentally innovative products, treating their employees extremely well, and additionally serving their community. Such goals may be compatible with a distant future or in a rigorously implemented market economy, a classless society, or a divinely created paradise. But in point of fact, these corporate goals are in competition with one another. The development of innovative products squeezes profits over the short term and thereby also decreases the chances of paying dividends, wages, or taxes. Raising stockholder dividends can often be achieved only at the expense of new product development, by lowering wages, or reducing tax payments.

Government subsidized theaters are, on the one hand, required to present attractive cultural programs for the largest possible number of citizens in the areas they serve. If possible, the house should sell out every night.

Achieving that kind of goal would be easily within reach if a municipal theater could use its public funding to produce nothing but musicals such as *The Lion King*. A full house would be guaranteed, and in good years money would even flow back into the city's coffers. On the other hand, municipal theaters are also charged with promoting innovative artistic works, and not infrequently this implies making concessions in terms of filling the hall or—from a cost-covering perspective—in terms of ticket prices. Directing a theater is an art unto itself, and it lies in managing such conflicting purposes in a way that the theater neither deteriorates into a production mill for Andrew Lloyd Webber musicals, nor is constantly required to request additional funding from the city.

Granted, there may be organizations that pursue only a single, clearly defined goal and, as a result, are in a position to optimize every decision with respect to achieving this end efficiently and effectively. But organizations normally strive to achieve a multitude of often contradictory goals, and this itself prevents the organization from becoming totally rationalized.

Goals as Window Dressing

As Niklas Luhmann recognized early on, all goals are not so instructive that they allow one to deduce the right, let alone the *only* right means to achieve them (see Luhmann, 1973a: 94). Slogans such as "the client is king," "humanize the workplace," "maximize profit," or "protect our environment" represent abstract behavioral expectations at best. The question of which behaviors are expected in a concrete situation is left unaddressed. If we are simply told, "Maximize everything that's good at the same time," we will have difficulty inferring instructions for handling specific situations. The slogan "protect our environment" is another example. How far should we take it? Would it also be permissible to kill somebody in an emergency? What are we expected to do if our actions line up with "the client is king," but they hurt other employees, the "company's most important capital resource?"

The formulation of somewhat abstract goals—one might also call them *values*—is often not at all intended to serve as a set of instructions for concrete actions but is aimed instead at gaining acceptance of the organization in its surroundings (see Meyer and Rowan, 1977: 340ff.; and very early Luhmann, 1964: 108ff.). If business executives in a capitalist economy do not aggressively affirm the goal of profit maximization they will presumably raise the hackles of their shareholders, just as a labor union functionary will run afoul of labor activists if she does not strive to achieve the objective of representing union members as effectively as possible, or at least communicate that she is doing so.

As a result, organizations often turn into veritable "affirmation machines," regularly embracing every conceivable social value that is in vogue but barely allowing them to influence their actions. Vocal, colorful declarations of belief in environmental protection, occupational safety, gender equality or the advancement of minorities are not automatically followed by appropriate steps.

On the contrary, the greater the opportunity to gain acceptance in the environment through abstract formulations of value, the greater the problems organizations encounter when these values are to be implemented in the form of concrete action (see Luhmann, 1982a: 26ff.). The problem is that the requirements of building external acceptance and the internal need to have the most precise decision-making instructions possible are as a rule mutually exclusive. Organizations usually solve this problem by doing both. They affirm a multitude of appealing values to the outside world, while internally setting clear goals that are at best only loosely associated with the values. These two strategies are incompatible, but that is another story.

Changing Goals

As organizational science recognized soon after the Second World War, goals do not offer a suitable point of departure for analyzing organizations. The reason is simple: even the "highest," "ultimate" goals can be modified (see Blau, 1955). Companies that initially manufactured rubber boots—such as the Nokia corporation, to cite one example—can alter their goal to that of producing gas masks and communication cables, and then to the development, assembly, and sale of mobile phones. Firms that primarily produce steel pipes modify their goal in such a way that they come to be viewed as experts in operating cellphone networks.

Naturally, organizations do not enjoy unlimited freedom to change their goals, if only because companies, public administrations, or hospitals have invested large sums of money to purchase machinery, provide training and professional development for their staff, or develop procedures, and therefore cannot retool for a different purpose without considerable disruption. It may be possible to beat swords into plowshares, but not into computers. With some effort, engineers can be retrained as call-center workers, but they can't be transformed into an elite combat unit. In this context, economists speak of "sunk costs"—resources that have already been spent on certain things and are simply no longer available for other purposes. Nonetheless, in spite of the commitments that organizations have entered through previous decisions, the speed at which they revamp their goals is fascinating.

Such goal changes often transpire unobserved by customers, employees, or suppliers and occasionally even by those at the top levels of the organization itself. At a first, superficial glance, we might characterize McDonald's as a chain of fried food outfits with the goal of selling hamburgers, French fries, and warm and cold caffeinated beverages as profitably as possible. In reality, McDonald's qualifies as one of the world's largest real estate lessors, with property holdings valued in excess of thirty billion dollars. The company's business model is based on making a piece of real estate available to small-business owners and then turning a profit on them, not only by collecting fees for the use of the McDonald's logo and selling them frozen ground meat patties, but primarily by charging them handsome rents and leasing fees. Harry J. Sonneborn, who was the gray eminence behind McDonald's chairman Ray Croc in the early days, once expressed it succinctly in a statement intended for banks. McDonald's, he said, was not a player in the fast food industry, but primarily active in the real estate sector instead.

There are many potential reasons for changing goals: new legislation, sudden changes in the priorities of management, the spin-off of individual departments, serendipitous innovations that occur as by-products of research intended for entirely different purposes and suddenly require a shift of attention, the achievement of a previously set goal, or the failure to accomplish one. It is worth examining some of the reasons for changing purposes in greater detail.

Reaching a Goal

Organizations frequently set themselves goals that can never be fully achieved. Advancing the salvation of souls as undertaken by the church, the education of children and adolescents, or the production of food products are goals that can never be accomplished once and for all. New sins are constantly committed, children are born in an unbroken stream, and feelings of hunger always re-emerge. Other organizations, in turn, have purposes that can actually be accomplished someday, such as the eradication of a disease, the realization of a supra-regional road construction project, the introduction of women's suffrage, or the eradication of an ethnic minority.

If organizations functioned merely as instruments to achieve goals—as the classical, purposive-rational perspective provides—then they would actually have to disband once the end has been met. Meanwhile, a large number of studies show that organizations continue to exist even when they have accomplished their original mission. It becomes apparent that after their goal has been reached, they unleash a large amount of motivation and creative thinking to discover which additional purposes they might serve.

The March of Dimes Foundation is an impressive example of such tenacity. Its original purpose was to fight polio. By staging huge events, the foundation solicited small amounts of money, i.e., dimes, which were then used to finance medical research on the disease. When a vaccine was discovered, polio was eradicated to a large degree, and the foundation's mission had been accomplished. But instead of disbanding, the organization set itself different goals such as discovering genetic defects in newborns and providing care for premature infants (see Sills, 1957). The March of Dimes was so effective as a fund-raising instrument and such a well-established "brand" with public donors that it apparently couldn't die. Rather than simply dissolving, the organization generated new goals in the form of supporting fundamental virological research, mapping out new professional education programs at medical universities, and developing measures to support the handicapped.

The Failure to Accomplish a Goal

When an organization has obviously accomplished its goal, one might argue that it should remain intact as a special purpose "task force." After all, it has already proven its efficiency. When an organization has patently failed to attain its goal, however, this argument is no longer sustainable. In spite of this, empirical research shows that organizations often survive even after they have clearly not succeeded.

Good examples of such persistence even in the face of obvious failure can be seen in organizations that are established to bring a major event to a city or country. To illustrate, five German cities, Düsseldorf, Frankfurt, Hamburg, Leipzig, and Stuttgart, competed to host the 2012 Olympic Games. One might assume that the agencies responsible for submitting the cities' tenders would have been disbanded no later than the point at which they were eliminated from the bidding process. Even though they were actually established for a highly specific project, the organizations in part continue to exist. They modified their goals in the direction of promoting their cities' overall sports landscape, marketing the city itself, or other forms of urban development. Once an organization has been founded, its tenacity and ability to generate imaginative new goals often appear to outweigh the disappointment over a clear failure to reach a goal.

One can also cite examples that sound abstruse at first, such as the case of a UFO sect surrounding Chicago housewife Marion Keech. After coming strongly under the influence of Church of Scientology founder and later science fiction writer Ron Hubbard, Keech announced that she had received a series of messages from outer space informing her that a major flood would inundate the earth on December 21, 1954. She was surrounded by a small circle of people who, according to the announcement, would be removed to the safety of outer space by a flying saucer before the flood. Social psychologists Leon Festinger, Henry Riecken, and Stanley Schachter, who allowed themselves to be recruited as members of the cult, watched as the scheduled time for the departure with the extraterrestrials passed, and the group was increasingly seized by despair. Marion Keech broke down and began to cry bitterly. The messages were read repeatedly to determine whether some important piece of information might have been overlooked. They resorted to and then rejected one explanation after the other for the visitors' failure to appear. Then, at 4:45 AM, Mrs Keech called the group together and announced that she had received a message. In the style of an Old Testament prophet, she proclaimed that God had saved the world from destruction because the group, after sitting together through the entire night, had spread so much light that it would not be water but rather light itself which inundated the earth. The UFO sect successfully survived the failure and subsequently attempted to recruit further supporters (see Festinger, Riecken, and Schachter, 1956).

One option seems to be recasting one's failure as a success by either modifying or forgetting the initial goals. Where this is impossible—for example, bidding to host the Olympic Games—the strategy appears to consist of identifying positive ancillary effects that justify the organization's continuing existence. Not infrequently, such attempted reinterpretations also receive outside encouragement, for example, because they enable the sponsors of a patently failed venture to prove that their financial support did not go to waste.

Reversing the End and the Means

According to the traditional, purposive-rational perspective, the means serve to achieve an organization's end. In practice, however, means often acquire a quality of their own. The ends for which the means were originally developed are forgotten, and the means themselves begin to be pursued with enthusiasm, as if they now represented the organization's goal. As a result, school examinations no longer function as a means of allowing pupils to monitor their learning progress, but instead become the very reason for learning. Getting together in church-sponsored youth groups, senior citizen meetings at the parish hall, and après-church service coffee klatches at some point no longer amounts to praising the Lord in the sense of "where two or three are gathered together in my name." Rather, the primary focus of the parish work has now shifted to socializing.

This kind of end-means reversal happens incrementally, with the effect that it barely comes to the attention of the organization itself. For many years, raising additional funds was viewed strictly as a means of financing expensive research at universities. It would not have occurred to anyone to confuse raising sums of money for research purposes with producing the scientifically interesting research findings themselves. Yet due to the search for quantifiable measures of successful research, attracting financial support often transforms itself from a means to an end. Even the fund-raising for a major project, for research in a particular area, or a cluster of researchers is now viewed as an indication of scientific excellence in its own right, well before the scientists deliver their actual findings. Accordingly, inquiries about the amount of funding secured—"How many millions have you generated in research funding?"—often appear to play a more important role in the application for professorships than the quality of the candidate's publications.

Frequently, this type of end-means reversal can only be observed and criticized from the outside. Criticism directed at healthcare organizations indicates that in treating their patients, they lose sight of their true purpose, namely, restoring health. Even though health is our goal, when we enter a hospital, rehabilitation facility, or specialist clinic, what we receive, so the accusation runs, are merely medical services. According to Ivan Illich (1975), not only doctors but also patients confuse the means (the provision of medical services) with the end. They overlook that more medical services often even lead to poorer health. From the patient's perspective, this can certainly be viewed as organizational "pathology," while from the perspective of organizational sociology, shifting attention away from intended purposes and refocusing it on procedures represents business as usual.

Seeking Goals After the Fact

Research on organizational decision processes has further radicalized criticism on the purposive-rational model. A company, public administration, or university will portray its decision-making processes to the outside world as if defining goals came first—through elaborate strategy processes, goal-setting workshops, or by virtue of a lone decision by the CEO—and all subsequent decisions were geared to achieving the goals. The suggestion is that goals and purposes come first, and then the actions.

While such cases no doubt occur, many times the goal is sought only after action has been taken. A large body of research on organizational decision making shows that organizations are constantly making decisions without always being clear about the basis or reason for them. Once a decision has produced an effect, the search begins for potential goals that might serve as suitable justification for the decision. According to organizational sociologist James G. March, organizational decision-making behavior involves not only the goal-oriented activity of the members, but also a continual process of finding goals to legitimize activities that have already occurred. In brief, the action often precedes the goal and the announcement of the goal is then often a justification of steps that have already been taken (March, 1976: 72).

Examples of such after-the-fact goal definitions can be observed in consulting projects where goals emerge only slowly. Companies, government agencies, and hospitals use tender documents and consulting contracts as a means of suggesting that they have a clear idea—even *before* they award the job—of the goals they want to achieve through the consultants' efforts. And some projects do adhere to the goals initially agreed upon. If the activity of the consultants produces unexpected effects, however, then goals must be sought to legitimize them after the fact. In the end, the purpose of the consulting project is reported to have been, say, to identify the need for further continuing education offerings, whereas the project was initially discussed within the context of performance-based compensation models.

Psychologist Karl Weick refers to this process of seeking goals after the fact as "sensemaking," in other words, the process of "making heads or tails out of something." According to Weick, the sense of an action or decision is frequently constructed retroactively because one generally doesn't discover what purpose an activity actually serves until it has been performed. The classic, fundamental idea—and this infuriates purposive-rationalists—could be formulated as: "How can I know what an organization's goals are, until I see which decisions are being made inside of it?" Weick concludes that the task of management lies not so much in defining appropriate goals and deducing the means to achieve them, but rather in creating a framework within which the many diverse decisions made in the organization can be interpreted and ordered (Weick, 1995: 9ff.).

Conclusion: Goals Represent One Structural Characteristic among Others

Adherents of the purposive-rational view needn't be confused by such manifold "contaminations" of their goal optimization-oriented image of organizations. If an organization continues to exist even though its founding goal has already been achieved, then one can assume negligence on the part of the supervisory agencies and demand that they show the courage to shut it down. If reversals of ends and means are observed, one can speak up during a strategy retreat and demand that the organization's original goals be recalled to mind. If focusing on two contradictory goals is standing in the way of thoroughly rationalizing operations, then that calls for a clear strategy specifying a split into two organizations, each with its own well-defined purpose.

In this manner, one can effectively use day-to-day organizational practice as an immunization against the various uncertainties of the classical model. The motto is: if reality doesn't line up with my PowerPoint slides and their simplified schemes of means and end, then that's too bad for day-to-day praxis. Managers, consultants, and researchers then take deviations as an occasion to demand clearer goals, unambiguous statements of purpose, or the elimination of all contradictory goals. The goal becomes a kind of fetish, which organizational analysis refuses to reject. As an outside observer, one is reminded of Sisyphus rolling a boulder up the hill of purposive rationality again and again, even though the stone repeatedly slips out of his hands. But if a heretical remark were permitted, one might note that it is precisely this eternal failure to meet one's own demands for rationality that keeps Sisyphus in motion—as well as providing employment for managers and consultants. And presumably, to a certain degree, it's a good thing.

Nevertheless, the picture turns into a caricature if one clings to the fetish idea that an organization can be completely brought into line with a goal. Admittedly, the portrayal of organizations as consisting of end-means relationships is simple, well laid out, and intelligible. It makes analyzing organizations relatively easy. Depending on the complexity of the problem, all one needs to calculate the right solution is a larger or smaller amount of computing power or a larger or smaller number of staff workers and research assistants. Yet this portrayal unfortunately has but little bearing on organizational reality.

A more productive approach used by the system theory is to inquire into the logic underlying all of these "contaminations" of the classical, purpose-based portrayal. Why does switching goals make sense? Why continue the organization irrespective of its failure or success in achieving its goals; and what good does it do to put the end before the means? What is the rationale for aligning an organization with several competing goals? Why is it impossible for organizations to dispense with the most appealingly worded statements possible, even though they do almost nothing to inform decision making?

Between Rigidity and Arbitrariness of Goals

Imagine that the dream of purposive-rationalists, namely, organizational alignment with a single goal, actually came true. You can use people as an example to illustrate the problem. This thought experiment asks the question: what would be the outcome if a person were to embrace only one single goal?

Presumably, the exclusive and rigid pursuit of a single goal would make a person go to pieces. A researcher who saw the sole meaning of her life in solving one of the world's scientific mysteries would at some point have to be put on artificial feeding because an occupation as banal as taking nutrition would seem unimportant to her. In a sense, she would be externally forced to take goals seriously. A man who thought only of sex and viewed every situation—issuing instructions at work, teaching university seminars, or agitating for a cause at a political convention—exclusively as an opportunity to recruit new sex partners would become a candidate for Sex Addicts Anonymous at some point, because his obsession with sex would be perceived as inappropriate in many situations.

Nevertheless, people cannot treat goals in a completely erratic fashion either. Goal rigidity can ruin a person, but people can also founder because they lack the ability to concentrate on one goal, and one goal only, for at least a short period of time. An employee who finds herself in a meeting devoted to positioning a new electric toothbrush will encounter acceptance problems if her attention continuously, not just occasionally, wanders to other interesting thoughts such as the romantic experiences of the night before, making a new Pac-Man record, or the dishwasher that still remains unloaded. Conversely, an executive who is having a romantic dinner with his new love interest will encounter acceptance problems if telephone calls, SMS messages, and e-mails continually remind him of his other responsibilities, and he is no longer certain which goal he should actually pursue.

In practical terms, *opportunistic goal setting* is predominant, in other words, more or less abruptly adjusting goals to suit existing opportunities and constraints (see Cyert and March, 1963: 35f. and 118; for greater detail see Luhmann, 1982a: 26ff. and Luhmann, 2010: 226ff.). Depending on which pressures or opportunities present themselves, one switches back and forth between different goals. If people happen to be in love, then they let work slide a little. By the same token, it's a well-known fact that the best books are written during phases when one is not distracted by the day-to-day chaos of a romance.

Goals Are One Option for Creating Structure

Goals represent one of the possible ways to program an organization—but only *one* of them. Goals can function as guiding parameters, for example, in the search for suitable personnel or for meaningful assignment within the organization. Yet it can also happen that one already has the employee and is looking for suitable tasks for her.

From this vantage point, the many deviations from a single-purpose orientation no longer appear to be pathological, as they do in the classic purposive-rational model, but rather as expressions of organizational adaptability. Thus, conscious or unconscious goal switching, the continuing existence of organizations regardless of their success or failure in achieving their goals, the reversal of ends and means, and the use of goals to justify decisions after the fact are exactly the times when—to use the big word—organizations express their "intelligence."

HIERARCHIES: AN ORGANIZATION'S "SACRED ORDER"

An organization's hierarchy is a feature that almost always immediately strikes the eye. Even a quick look at the corporate chart of Deutsche Bank shows that the divisions, departments, and groups are hierarchically ordered. In the US Army, there were twenty-six different ranks in the hierarchy for a time, from the simple private, the so-called E1, to the five-star general, a position held to date only by George Washington and Dwight D. Eisenhower. And a number of government developmental aid organizations that praise themselves for their flat hierarchies have more than eight hierarchical levels, even by a conservative count, for their 5,000 employees.

Hierarchy was long accepted without criticism as the central management and coordinating mechanism for companies, government agencies, the military, hospitals, prisons, universities, schools, and, to a lesser extent, for associations, political parties and organizations as well. With the exception of isolated attempts at democratization launched in some organizations, particularly during the second half of the twentieth century, hierarchies were viewed for a long time as *the* management tool to link complex decision-making processes to one another. Acceptance was not limited to the actual hierarchs, that is, executives themselves. The majority of employees—whose role in a company was restricted to receiving instructions and carrying them out—also accepted the central importance of hierarchical structures. In its importance as a "sacred order" (as the word is translated literally) hierarchy does honor to its name in operational practice. In that sense, it would almost seem logically consistent that an entire organization would sometimes be portrayed as a hierarchy.

If the principle of a hierarchical system is somewhat frowned upon in a society oriented on the equal status of all citizens, then why do hierarchies play a role in organizations at all? Why is it that hierarchical differentiation between higher and lower emerges even in self-governing companies no later than the point at which they consist of 25 employees? If the large-scale, state-socialist experiments conducted in the Soviet Union and Eastern Europe were ultimately based on the idea that all citizens were equal, then why then did they not abandon hierarchical principles in their plants, government administrations, hospitals, or universities?

Hierarchy Stabilizes Management

Theoretically, one could leave the development of organizational leadership to the free play of forces. Each new decision could entail a further round of jockeying for rank, in which case employees would have to justify why they were laying claim to a leadership role under the given circumstances. Depending on the particular matter at hand, first one, then another employee might assume leadership. Yet rather than assigning leadership roles on a case-by-case basis, organizations tend to define stable hierarchies.

As a rule, hierarchies are established for an unlimited term. There are models that involve temporarily stepping in for a superior, interim management, or assuming management tasks on a limited-term basis. But in general, every member of an organization can assume that the hierarch of today will still be the hierarch of tomorrow. No one is surprised when today's manager quite naturally asks her assistant for a cup of coffee the following morning. And for the members of the organization who assume leadership roles, it is clear that by accepting a position of that kind they "must permanently and consciously behave like leaders from that point on" (Luhmann, 1964: 208).

Furthermore, hierarchies determine precisely who is subordinate to whom. The hierarchical structure underlying an organizational chart regulates the decisive social relationships within the entity and thereby contributes to coordinating the behavior of individual members (see Luhmann, 1964: 209). Certainly, there will occasionally be employees who don't know exactly who they have been assigned to, and there are phases during which superiors argue over who is in charge of certain employees. Be that as it may, one generally observes that such ambiguity of assignment is quickly resolved. If confusion or inconsistency in the assignment of employees continues, it is the task of the superior to set the matter in order again.

In addition, hierarchies distribute functional responsibilities—not only horizontally among departments at the same level, but also vertically between the various hierarchical ranks. In principle, meanwhile, the option of moving any topic up to a higher level remains intact. While it is true that hierarchs will take the step of assuming decentralized responsibilities only under extraordinary circumstances, in principle they always retain the option and the formal right to appropriate any decision situation below their station and to declare that a problem area is "a matter for the boss."

Accepting the Hierarchy as a Condition of Membership

A leadership structure acquires stability because accepting it is made a condition of membership. When one joins an organization, and wishes to remain there, one must accept the instructions of one's superiors even if they don't seem particularly meaningful. People who wish to experience the potency of this mechanism for themselves need only conduct a simple crisis experiment. They can simply tell a superior that in the future they are no longer willing to take orders—and then wait to see the reaction.

Acceptance of the hierarchy as a condition of membership has an important effect. In the final analysis, when making decisions superiors do not need to rely on the respect of their subordinates as a basis of support (see Luhmann, 1964: 209). A commander can send his troops into battle without having to be at the front line himself to motivate them. Superiors do not need to supply their employees with clear explanations of the rationale for their instructions in each and every instance—be it carrying out a risky military operation, the expensive process of developing a new sandwich spread, or the legally contentious pursuit of copyright pirates. This enables the organization to place people in hierarchical positions who are indeed professionally qualified but are not endowed with any particular charisma.

This notion—relief from the burden of acquiring the respect of subordinates—gives rise to vehement protest among the readers and writers of modern management literature. When Jeff Bezos, founder and long-standing chairman of Internet mail order business Amazon, and his managers help out on the assembly lines in his logistics centers during the Christmas season, then that is taken as a clear indication of how important it is to be a model for one's subordinates. Management literature would suggest that a senior officer who is respected only because of her position in the hierarchy but not as a human being will be unable to function effectively. The entire body of organizational experience, this camp maintains, demonstrates that whenever instructions are given they must always be presented to subordinates as convincingly reasonable.

To be sure, there is little to be said against employees having respect for their superiors in a personal sense as well, or against employees carrying out orders in the conviction that they are correct. Often, however, this is only possible when fair weather conditions prevail, in other words, when business is good, no drastic cuts are required, and the employees feel secure in their jobs. But organizations could not survive over the long term if their members were willing to comply only if they immediately understood the sense of an order or if they were swept away by their superiors.

If the creation of a hierarchy relieves executives of the necessity to garner the respect of their employees, which possibilities emerge?

Alignment with the Demands of the Environment

In idealized conceptions of organizations, an orientation based on the market, the "people," or on the law is always paired with a focus on the happiness of each individual employee. From their soapboxes, corporate CEOs or the heads of government agencies proclaim that the most important tools for achieving customer satisfaction are their own inspired and inspiring employees. And even labor unions proclaim— shifting the focus of the argumentation somewhat—that corporations, public administrations, prisons, or the military can only achieve their goals if their employees are both adequately compensated for their work and feel comfortable in the organization as well.

But life in organizations is no bed of roses. The attitudes and stances of managers cannot be geared primarily to employees in a benevolently authoritarian way, but must instead remain focused on the demands of customers, clients, or the electorate (Luhmann, 1964: 210). And the demands impinging on an organization from without are frequently at cross purposes with those advanced from the inside, that is, from the employees. Clients want to buy services at the best price possible, while employees want to receive decent wages for their work. Customers demand a contact person—ideally available at all times—while employees want to go home at some point.

Hierarchies enable organizations to adapt to the specific demands of their surroundings without having to make allowances in every case for their members' sensitivities. Corporations can ponder which markets they would like to conquer, without being forced to consider whether their employees would actually be willing to transfer to the region in question. Churches can deliberate which doctrines are best suited to win and retain believers, without immediately doubting the willingness of their full-time professional staff to comply every time a decision is made.

The Ability to Impose the Unaccustomed

In their self-presentations, many organizations advance the idea that all of their employees should be able to recognize the rationality of modifications which have become "necessary due to changing conditions in the environment." As a result, they spend large amounts of time promoting their new orientations or justifying their reasons for spinning off a corporate unit. Yet almost all empirical studies show that the ability to increase acceptance through reasoning runs up against its limitations, particularly when profound changes are involved.

Since hierarchies make it superfluous for executives to rely on the personal respect of their employees for support, management is able to make unpopular decisions that disappoint the expectations employees have held until that time (see Luhmann, 1964: 209). Executives can transfer production units to foreign countries without presupposing that the affected employees will accede. Managers can introduce new production methods even if it means devaluing the skills of long-standing employees, and they can begin with the development and sale of contentious products such as intermediate-range missiles, nuclear fuel rods, or non-returnable bottles without having to show deference to their members' religious or moral sensitivities.

The ability of hierarchs to initiate new beginnings in some organizations stands in particularly stark contrast to organizations that can fall back on hierarchies only to a limited degree. For example, the latter may do without hierarchies out of political conviction, or because they are not in a position to pay their members and therefore cannot demand that they subordinate themselves to a hierarchy. Empirical research shows that organizations of this kind tend to be oriented toward maintaining the status quo; fundamental change is the very thing that poses enormous difficulty for them. Meanwhile, organizations with pronounced hierarchies can transform themselves profoundly with greater ease and do so more often (see March and Simon, 1958: 194ff.).

Cracks in the Hierarchy

The central role of hierarchies promoted the emergence of hero-oriented management approaches that cast organizational success or failure as the result of actions undertaken by individual executives. One need only examine the biographies of corporate leaders such as General Electric CEO Jack Welch, military leaders like Dwight D. Eisenhower, or politicians like John F. Kennedy. Ultimately these stories revolve around heroic men, and increasingly women, who had all the answers and could resolve any problem. True, the heroic tales always find due praise for the contributions of the simple worker, the simple soldier, or the simple department head, but ultimately the organizations are portrayed as hierarchies that were adeptly run by managers at the top.

Yet hierarchical reality differs from what the heroic accounts of organizations would have us believe.

Information from the Environment Accrues Not Only at the Top: The Influence of Organizational Interfaces

The classical concept of a hierarchical structure implies that the top echelons of an organization can monopolize relevant interactions with the external world (Luhmann, 1982a: 31ff.). But monopolizing external communications at the top presumably only works in the smallest of organizations, where every letter—as a symbol for external contact—still crosses the boss's desk for her personal signature. Under such circumstances, it may still be possible for every client to speak with the manager directly, or for her to be involved in every conversation with suppliers or partners and handle all contacts with state and local authorities herself.

The larger an organization becomes, the more external contacts must be delegated. Interfaces with customers, suppliers, partners, or the media are distributed widely across the entire organization. A company's important customers are no longer serviced by the chief executive but rather by so-called "key account managers." Press officers are often aware that "something's cooking" before their superiors because they—as opposed to their managers—stem from the same milieu as the journalists who are researching the organization.

Those who are situated at organizational interfaces can use their direct contacts with the environment to increase their influence (see Crozier and Friedberg, 1979: 51f.). They can spread information about what the organization's partners are supposedly thinking. Their privileged contacts with suppliers, partners, or customers put them in a position to drop hints that an important partner would undoubtedly pull out if the organization were to pursue a certain strategy. This, in turn, gives them a chance to float their own preferred plans of action.

Executives may strive to have the information that accumulates at organizational interfaces channeled "upstairs," not only so that they themselves have access to the knowledge, but also to curtail the influence of the employees at the interfaces. According to this line of thinking, all relevant information should come together at the top. Elaborate computer-based management information systems are installed which will supposedly enable top management to control all pertinent information—the way it is in an airplane cockpit. With that in mind, sometimes sizeable administrative departments are established to compile information for top executives and process it into digestible, bite-sized pieces. The entire organization is trained in composing brief summaries or at most one page opinions that keep top executives well informed on the one hand, while not completely inundating them with information on the other.

Nevertheless, in spite of the management information systems, the administrative units, and training the staff to write brief summaries, information received at the various organizational interfaces is always reported to higher levels with some delay. Henry Ford, founder of the Ford Motor Company and one of the twentieth century's trailblazing management thinkers, explained that there is nothing more dangerous than the clear, elaborately designed communication channels suggested by a corporate organizational chart. Such charts, he said, were laid out in the form of trees with "nice little clusters" hanging on them, each bearing the name of the person in charge. But it took six weeks for news about a person in the lower left corner to reach the chairman of the board (as quoted in Milgrom and Roberts, 1992: 4).

Frequently, as information passes through an organization it is repeatedly changed and modified (see Luhmann, 2010: 202). At every step along the way, something is added, altered, or shortened so that by the time the information reaches the executive suite it often bears little resemblance to its original form. One need only speak with an administrative employee who happens to come across a note that she had originally drafted and now barely recognizes after its transformation at the next higher levels of the hierarchy. It is all somewhat reminiscent of the children's game of "telephone," where the original message is no longer intelligible by the time it arrives at the end of the line.

Particularly when information is problematic—for example, when it involves the threat of losing a customer, problems with suppliers, or an impending change in legislation—subordinate employees are often reluctant to feed it into the information system along with all its drama. In many cases there is a frequently not unjustified expectation that the person who will "have his head taken off" is ultimately not the one responsible for the bad news but the one who conveys it. Since many top managers, be it in the military, the corporate world, or a government agency, proceed under the assumption that they are operating in an open communication environment, these filtering processes go entirely unnoticed. Unbeknownst to the executives themselves, those at the top have only a vague idea of what is actually transpiring in their organization's surroundings.

Subordinates Often Have Greater Expertise Than Their Superiors: The Influence of Experts

According to the classical concept of hierarchical organizations, rank corresponds of necessity to professional expertise. In an emergency, the person responsible for human resources—at least in this view—would also be able to handle payroll accounting, process travel costs, flex-time records, and severance pay, and would naturally also be conversant with the requisite personnel administration software. A head of state—again, according to this theory—would be so knowledgeable about the various aspects of foreign, domestic, judicial, education, finance, developmental, and economic policy that she could not only assess the competence of her ministers, but also manage their ministries if the need arose.

Nevertheless, the specialization that establishes itself in most organizations makes it unlikely that superiors are as well informed as their subordinates in all areas. The demands arising in a given area of operations become so diverse that no single person is master of them all, not even the chief. As a result, hierarchical authority and professional expertise diverge (see Thompson, 1961: 485ff.).

Of course, management can attempt to centralize expertise. Labor unionist and journalist Harry Braverman observed—entirely in keeping with the tradition of Karl Marx—that in businesses as well as government agencies, hospitals, and educational institutions increasingly prevalent rationalization strategies serve to heighten the separation of work process from the experience, knowledge, and traditions of the craftsman's abilities. The know-how that workers have acquired over decades and centuries is systematically being transferred to management. Braverman suspects that the intention lies in ending dependency on the qualifications of the worker, thereby allowing organizations to make their members entirely subservient to management's goals, ideas, and plans (see Braverman, 1974: 124ff.).

Yet in spite of the efforts to document in writing the entire stock of necessary knowledge, the installation of central computer databanks, and using process software à la SAP to manage the whole organization, such attempts have met with only limited success. Storing knowledge in a central location assumes that the facts and circumstances are easily documentable, whereas in reality much information emerges in highly ambivalent, context-dependent forms and is difficult to record (Luhmann, 2000: 86). Much of an organization's knowledge exists only in the shadows surrounding central databanks, and even if one were to succeed in compiling the greater part of the information in such form, presumably only a small number of people would know how to access what is relevant. In actual fact, pertinent information will always be available only at isolated locations, and these will not necessarily be found at the top levels of the hierarchy.

Technical knowledge is a source of influence for employees. To illustrate, in a well-known study of the French, state-run tobacco industry by organizational sociologist Michel Crozier, it emerged clearly that technical maintenance workers enjoyed a dominant power position; they were the only ones capable of repairing the highly complex machinery. To a large extent, therefore, they could determine on their own how often the machines malfunctioned, who would receive preferential treatment in matters of repair, and, if such a situation were to arise, how long it would take until production resumed. In practical terms, this knowledge gave them greater influence than the shop stewards or even central management whose goals were determined externally. Production methods, meanwhile, were to a large extent fixed, and the powerful unions made it virtually impossible to fire or replace personnel (see Crozier, 1963: 79ff.). As philosopher Francis Bacon commented at the end of the sixteenth century, "Knowledge is power."

Controlling Informal Communication Channels: The Influence of Gatekeepers

According to classical thinking, inner-organizational communication channels are controlled by the hierarchy. Superiors are thought to determine who should have access to whom, who should confer with whom, and which contacts should be forborne. Nevertheless, parallel to the communication channels controlled by the hierarchy, communication repeatedly flows along "beaten paths" which have *not* been mapped out by the hierarchy. One need only think of a brief exchange between employees from two different departments which occurs in the coffee kitchen, or the contacts that exist only because two people were in the same training class decades before, or the opportunities for communication that arise simply because one happens to find oneself in a location where various streams of information merge.

There is a tendency for those at the top of the hierarchy to formalize or at least influence such informal communications. Executives have now begun to attend special management seminars on the art of storytelling so that they can anchor a tale of success, an important lesson, or a particular perspective in the organization's informal communications. In the meantime, one of the main tasks of public relations departments appears to consist of familiarizing employees and outsiders with "stories" about top executives. The first organizations have now started actively managing rumors so that they can control internal talk and gossip.

All of these attempts seem fairly powerless, however. It is true that some employees will listen with rapt attention to the stories their superiors have developed in storytelling seminars, yet most of them will simply be amused. There is a possibility that employees will studiously spread the rumors set in motion from above. But the very opposite can occur as well, with rumor management resulting only in mistrust among the staff. Informal communication channels are not the outcome of decisions taken at the top echelons. They arise instead as a gradual, unnoticeable, and continuous process.

Knowing how to work an organization's informal communication channels is an asset the "little man" and "little woman" can exploit. The person who controls the rumors, talk, and gossip controls important communication channels.

The Special Characteristics of Influence Stemming from Beyond the Hierarchy

The sources of the influence wielded by employees on the lower rungs of the hierarchy can in substantial part be traced to the organization itself. It may, of course, be the case that an outside sales representative enjoys an excellent pre-existing relationship with a customer, and was perhaps even hired for that very reason. Frequently, though, the positive relationships have arisen only through activity at an organizational interface. In the same way, expertise on the mechanics of the equipment, software quirks, or the specific nature of chemical processes may have been acquired prior to joining the organization, say, as part of a person's education. But the knowledge that is relevant for the organization often results from years of actually working on site. Even if informal contacts can occasionally be traced to outside contacts—attending the same university, membership in a fraternity, or playing basketball on weekends—personal networks generally consist of people who did not know one another before coming on board.

Although these sources of influence are materially based on position within the organization, the organization cannot simply withdraw them. Managers at the top cannot simply bundle up the good relationships prevailing at many of the interfaces and incorporate them into headquarters. The employees' expertise cannot simply be taken away from them again. Forcing them to share it works only to a limited degree. The communication channels that lie outside of the formal structure elude the influence of the hierarchy as well. Good external relations, expertise on the way things work, and contacts inside the organization are instruments of labor that are of necessity private property and, in contrast to other business resources such as computers, machinery, or buildings, cannot simply be converted into property of the organization (see Luhmann, 1982a: 31ff.).

Conclusion: The Surveillance of Employees from Above, and the Sousveillance of Superiors from Below

The frequently extreme importance of external contacts at (hierarchically speaking) very low-level interfaces, the expertise found at the bottom of the organization, and the control exerted by simple employees over informal communication channels, have the effect that the formal hierarchy as it emerges from an organizational chart is rarely a true reflection of the relationships of influence. Many times, formally allocated authority and actual influence on decision making diverge significantly. As a result, one often has the impression that—to quote a bon mot by Niklas Luhmann—organizations are characterized not only by the "surveillance of subordinates" but also by more or less efficient "sousveillance of superiors."

How the "Sousveillance" of Superiors Functions

As a rule, the "sousveillance" of a superior is not the result of intrigue, an attempt to "cut the legs off his chair," or an expression of personal antipathy. On the contrary, organizations can often function only if superiors are effectively sousveilled. After all, superiors have only twenty-four hours a day at their disposal (time limitations), only a limited number of contact opportunities (social limitations), and only a relatively small amount of "gray matter"—at least in comparison to the vast number of employees below them (factual limitation). From a sousveillance perspective, it makes sense to examine these three limitations.

In terms of the *factual dimension*, compiling all of the relevant information on their own is often an overwhelming task for superiors. They therefore assign the job to their subordinates. Subordinates, in turn, use the conveyance of information to exert substantial influence over their superiors' decision-making process. The kind of information they gather, consider relevant, and pass along to higher levels influences whether one decision is more likely than another. The subordinate's motto reads: As long as I'm allowed to compile the information, the boss is welcome to make the decision and assume the responsibility for its implementation (see Luhmann, 1982a: 31f.).

As a result, directives are frequently not conceived up above and then handed down out of a clear blue sky in the form of orders, instructions, or requests. Instead, often enough they simply represent formalizations of what had already been planned at lower levels. To illustrate, we now know that decisions pertaining to the bureaucratic planning of the annihilation of Jews during the Nazi regime were often prepared at very low administrative levels of the Reich Main Security Office, before Reinhard Heydrich or Heinrich Himmler ("up above") signed off on them as a formality. Key documents—for example, instructions to prepare "a final solution of the Jewish question," the invitation to attend the planning of the final solution at the Wannsee Conference, or, in Adolf Eichmann's department, the order to prevent the emigration of Belgian and French Jews—were first drawn up in the Reich Main Security Office and then signed by the top officers of the Reich (see Lozowick, 2000: 73f.).

In terms of the *social dimension*, the options of superiors for maintaining contacts within the organization are also limited. Executives do not have enough contact surfaces to satisfy all the demands from their subordinates, colleagues, or their own superiors, let alone those of people outside the organization. As an illustration, one need only consider how short on time superiors appear in the eyes of their subordinates, and how grateful superiors often are when their subordinates keep appointments brief, cancel meetings, or even take appointments off their hands. This is why it makes sense when collaborating with others, to use official channels as little as possible and instead have low-level units draw up solutions which are then simply presented to the respective managers for approval.

We know from organizational research on government ministries that senior officers have a preference for "coordinated documents." Ministry employees try to orient themselves according to the presumed intentions and evaluation criteria of the executive staff, but because this form of coordination requires that all of the departments are in agreement, what frequently emerge are decisions based on the smallest common denominator. Then, rather than unraveling a laboriously negotiated interdepartmental compromise, the minister signs off on this smallest common denominator. Political scientist Fritz Scharpf (1993) refers to this as a "negative coordination," that is, an arrangement where each unit examines only whether the decision alternatives under consideration would negatively affect the status quo, and in the end the option is chosen which entails the least pain for everyone.

When it comes to the *time dimension*, employees in public administration, businesses, or hospitals frequently experience that executives are always unavailable just when one needs them to sign an important document, resolve a conflict, or appease a disgruntled customer. In the classic scenario, superiors function as the organizational eye of the needle through which all decisions must pass, even under time pressure. As a reaction, manifold attempts are undertaken to control the executive's time and therefore also to conduct the sousveillance in that regard. Secretaries schedule superiors' appointments. The higher people climb on the hierarchical ladder, the less autonomy they actually appear to have over their time.

The realization of the pivotal role played by the sousveillance of superiors has meanwhile contributed significantly to the fact that the notion of hierarchs as heroes of the organization is now viewed as more or less deliberately cultivated mythology. Today, in contrast, notions of "post-heroic management" seem to be gaining currency (see Handy, 1989). In simplified terms, this means that the task of management lies in developing employees in such a way that they can solve their own problems. Yet in many cases this merely involves a variation on the heroic manager theme—just that the hero now appears in the role of coach, mentor, or enabler who willingly shares the victory with "his" employees. In an advanced version, post-heroic management means that superiors allow leadership to filter up from below and are aware of their limitations.

Many times, newly minted executives in particular have not yet mastered the technique of allowing themselves to be efficiently sousveilled by their employees. They have been shaped by the autobiographies of great corporate leaders, spoiled by classical management theory as it continues to be taught in many MBA mills, and influenced by the mantra espoused by a number of purported management gurus who argue that there should at long last be less management and more leadership in organizations. As a result, new managers still associate leadership primarily with direction from the top down. Yet employees have a wide range of possibilities to discipline their superiors in such a way that they accept sousveillance.

One proven method is to make the executive's world grow smaller by regulating the flow of information. Sometimes all it takes is not (or not immediately) routing one piece of critical information upwards to make a minister, CEO, or chief administrator realize that she cannot do without information that has been processed by subordinates. Sometimes it may become necessary to systematically cut off superiors from information flows and to act dumb even in response to an explicit inquiry (see Luhmann, 1962: 22).

Conversely, one can also allow the complexity overhead to escalate. Executives are dependent on having as many decisions as possible reached or at least prepared in a decentralized manner, because the technical competence to do so is present only at lower levels. If a superior has a tendency to monopolize decision making, subordinates can demonstrate the effect this will have by approaching her for decisions on every single matter. A frequent outcome is an explosion of complexity at the top, which can only be remedied by extending the executive's work day or—if her work day cannot be extended any further—by accepting sousveillance by her employees.

Even though research in organizational science supports extolling post-heroic management, we must not forget the function served by a hierarchy.

How the Surveillance of Subordinates Functions

In principle, one can imagine a wide variety of ways to create binding decisions in organizations on a collective basis. One can discuss a matter until everyone agrees, be it because they have mutually convinced each other through "domination-free discourse," or because exhaustion leaves them no strength to insist on their original positions (see Habermas, 1981, who inclines toward the first variant). Or one can put different alternatives to a vote and then decide in favor of the approach preferred by the majority. A further option—which is said to arise particularly in illegal organizations such as the Hells Angels, the Mafia, or terrorist organizations—is to follow the person who is willing to impose his claim to leadership through physical violence toward all others. Nevertheless, in most organizations the central means of establishing decidability is through the hierarchy, and acceptance of the hierarchy has been flagged as a condition of membership.

Members of the hierarchy can resolve open decision-making situations simply by referring to their role as superiors. Upon entering an organization, individuals declare that they agree not only with the tasks they will be expected to perform, but also that they will submit to the hierarchy. Their superiors can therefore expect compliance and—in the event it is not forthcoming—place an individual's membership in question. As a consequence, organizations can create an impressive degree of decidability which applies to all members, encompasses all of the relevant issues, and can transpire very quickly should the need arise.

When a hierarchical organizational chart unequivocally sets forth who is subordinate to whom, this allows all organizational questions—in the *factual dimension*—to be led to a provisional resolution. Ultimately, anything that is vague, contradictory, or ambiguous can be pushed up to a higher level until it arrives at a point where somebody puts it in order again. To illustrate, from this perspective the interesting thing about the Cuban Missile Crisis of 1962 was that in the end the US reaction to the installation of Soviet atomic missiles on the Caribbean island was formulated by the president. Naturally, the Pentagon had drawn up three alternative reaction plans—a naval blockade, targeted air attacks on the rocket installations, or a large-scale land invasion—thereby limiting the president's options as commander-in-chief. And even though analyses of the event emphasize that the decisions of the Kennedy administration were somewhat arbitrary and haphazard in nature, the crisis itself is a good example of a topic being jacked up to a higher level in the hierarchy and thereby made decidable (see Allison, 1969).

On the *social dimension*, the hierarchy represents a mechanism to temporarily mitigate, although perhaps not to resolve, any conflict between parties in the organization. Whereas an argument in a discotheque, within a clique, or between a couple often can in the end be resolved only through separation, violence, or intervention by the authorities, organizations have the option of resolving interpersonal conflict by falling back on the hierarchy. Since every member of the organization is, as a rule, integrated into the hierarchy, in principle all personal conflict falls under the purview of a superior. If a conflict should escalate, a superior can invoke her authority and declare the matter decided. Thus, the hierarchy frees the people involved from the necessity of solving the problem by conducting resource-consuming power games to clarify ambiguous circumstances. Putting it differently, hierarchy translates the unrest of a personal pecking order into an order based on social comparison to which all parties are bound by the terms of membership (see Luhmann, 1975a: 52).

If necessary, decision making—this is the temporal dimension—can occur very quickly because superiors can compel their employees to accept choices immediately. The search for decisions can be shortened to comments such as: "Thank you for your opinion. In my capacity as your supervisor, I have decided that we'll handle the matter in such and such a way."

In the final analysis, superiors are justified in expecting that their own timelines will be adopted in the decision-making process. This makes decision making possible in a way that conserves resources because—in contrast to consensus or violence—it prevents laborious negotiation processes.

The ability of superiors to compel their employees to accept their choices rests on the fact that acceptance of the hierarchy is a condition of membership. Thus, the central mechanism superiors use to impose their decision consists of their "expulsion power" (see Luhmann, 1975a: 104ff.). Often, all it takes is a slight allusion from a superior—although sometimes a reprimand is required—to remind members that their presence in the organization is conditional. And not least among those conditions is accepting the decisions of one's superior.

The problem is that the threat of termination, which is to say, the use of "expulsion power," is a very blunt instrument. Thus, one draws on additional means to stimulate compliance in subordinates. "Career power," that is, the ability to influence a subordinate's advancement, is a much more subtle means than "expulsion power." Here, it is a question of passing a person over when there is a new position to be filled, or transferring someone to a position that is equal in a formal sense although somewhat less attractive (see Luhmann, 1975a: 104). Superiors can also bring their "resource power" to bear, for example, by throttling the resources subordinates need to perform their jobs. Ultimately, superiors also wield "informal power," for example, in the sense that they can show a greater or lesser degree of tolerance when their subordinates break the rules.

Hierarchies Involve a Dual Power Process

A good number of organizations have adopted the creed, succinctly stated, that hierarchy should be abolished. Whereas such demands were initially heard primarily in self-managed companies and grassroots political organizations, they now are also increasingly surfacing in for-profit businesses which appear to be moving away from strict, hierarchical decision-making structures. Not infrequently, management consultants are playing the same tune. For example, management guru and best-selling author Tom Peters raises the demand that hierarchies be torn down, disassembled, and hacked to pieces. A mortal blow to hierarchy has been announced: it will be delivered in the form of lean management, cost/profit center structures, and project management. Hierarchy is being described as a "model that is being discontinued." And yet the more stridently management literature discredits hierarchy, the more stubbornly organizational hierarchies seem to persist.

Rather than declaring that hierarchy is in crisis and finds itself in a cul-de-sac, and perhaps even proclaiming its demise—or doing the diametric opposite, namely, singing its praises—the point of interest appears to be that hierarchies create opportunities for both subordinates and superiors to influence one another. Contrary to first impressions, organizational science now realizes that hierarchies create opportunities that allow power to be exerted both from the top down as well as from the bottom up.

The dual power process involved in hierarchies, that is, influence exerted from above as well as from below must not lead to the faulty conclusion that the power distribution between superiors and subordinates is symmetrical. Sociologists Michel Crozier and Erhard Friedberg (1979: 40f.) have pointed out that while both sides in fact have something to offer in hierarchical relationships, one side always stands to gain somewhat more than the other depending on the power sources it controls. Naturally, the asymmetrical distribution of power often favors those who hold the higher rank. The relationship between a supermarket branch manager and her sales clerks, between a non-commissioned officer and a private in the army, or between the sole owner of a company and her employees will serve as examples. Often however, employees located at lower levels can gain considerable influence. One need only call to mind the employees with exclusive specialized know-how, the gray eminences in the central offices of political parties who know how to make various factions coalesce, or university professors who are secure in their positions based on lifetime contracts, but place greater value on having a good reputation in the scientific community than in the eyes of a dean or the president of the university.

One can attempt to examine power relationships that have been shaped by hierarchies and see which side is in the better position to profit. But this is only of interest if one is trying to learn whether there is any chance of "pushing something through" or, as the ultimate question, whether or not it is worth one's while to remain involved in a hierarchical relationship. In terms of an overarching understanding of the way hierarchies work, it is of greater interest to observe that the inverse proportionality of the dual power processes within a hierarchical framework—from the top down, as well as from the bottom up—makes a considerable contribution to the efficiency of organizational performance.

CHAPTER 3

MACHINES, GAMES, AND FAÇADES: THE THREE ASPECTS OF AN ORGANIZATION

Researchers use a wide range of analogies to characterize organizations, referring to them as trash cans, market places, data processing machines, or octopuses. They are compared to space ships and brains. Associations with beehives or prisons are evoked. *Images of Organizations*, to quote the title of a book by US organizational sociologist Gareth Morgan (1986), can be used to illustrate the differences between organizations. For example, a major corporation that is precisely programmed from start to finish and therefore reminiscent of a symphony orchestra can be distinguished from a somewhat more flexible and decentralized organization that might be compared to a jazz band, or a growth company that is constantly breaking the rules and in some respects reminds one of a rock group. Meanwhile, the organizational charts of administrations, corporations, or associations prompt us to think of organizations in terms of pyramids, onions, or trumpets, depending on how many echelons the hierarchy comprises and how broad or narrow a range of middle management functions appears on the diagram.

Specifically, there are three types of metaphors that play a central role in organizational research. Each of them focuses on a different aspect of organizations. Characterizing an organization as a *machine* highlights the predictability of the organization's processes. On the other hand, using the image of a game, as distinct from the metaphor of a machine, indicates that an organization is bustling with life—namely, beyond its official body of rules and regulations. By seeing organizations as *façades* observers underscore the importance of mobilizing support for an organization in its external environment by presenting a polished image to the outside world. These three metaphors in particular merit a somewhat closer examination.

Metaphors for the Three Aspects of Organizations

The *machine* metaphor addresses the predictable aspects of organizations. Much like machines, organizations consist of precisely defined individual elements, with each individual component performing a clearly delimited function in the overall machine. The individual parts only become meaningful through their integration in the total operation. Without such integration, an individual component loses its function. All of the gears in the organization have to mesh, as if it were a machine. The task of the machine operator, one might also use the term manager, is to set the wheels in motion and control them. Organizations, and machines as well, can consist of a vast number of individual parts and linkages, but ultimately their complexity can be managed by using precise descriptions of the processes involved. The operating manual for the machine, which is to say, the organizational handbook, simply becomes correspondingly thicker (see Ward, 1964: 37ff.).

Using the *game* analogy underscores the character of an organization as a field of resourceful activity where exploiting opportunity, a "willingness to take risks the enjoyment of variation, and surprises play important roles. Much like competitive games, organizations are said to be characterized by conflict between freedom and constraint, calculability and spontaneity, randomness and regularity, creativity and conventionality, competition and cooperation, and fairness and deception" (Neuberger, 1990: 163). Games are based on incomplete information and therefore require feinting and bluffing. They will often allow several solutions or even tolerate stalemate situations, and, in the final analysis, they are unjust because the rules of the game put some of the players at a distinct advantage. Social psychologist Karl Weick compares organizations with a game played on a round, sloped field with a large number of goals. Various individuals—although not everyone, of course—can enter or leave the game. They can throw new balls into the game, or they can attempt to remove them from the field. Everyone tries to kick or throw the balls into one of the goals, but every time he scores he has to be extremely careful that he also receives recognition for the goal. It reminds one a bit of the animals' soccer match in Walt Disney's *Bedknobs and Broomsticks* (see Weick, 1976: 1ff.).

The *façade* of a house is its visible side. Its purpose is to make an impression through ornaments or decoration or even simply through its regularity. It is intended for the public. The façade, as a saying goes, is "a present for the street" (see Rottenburg, 1996: 191ff.). There are windows in the façade so that the inhabitants can look out, but also so that the public can catch a glimpse of the inside. But even the windows are decorated with pretty curtains that can be closed quickly in an emergency. We speak of window dressing or decorative window treatments. This image suggests that organizations strive to make as favorable an impression as possible on the outside world in order to gain the approval of their clients, create a positive attitude toward themselves in the mass media, or acquire legitimacy in political circles. Granted, whatever is going on in "the back of the store" is not entirely unimportant, but appropriately sprucing up the façade and its display windows has a significant effect on the survival of the organization.

Specializations on One Aspect

The metaphors of the machine, the game, and the façade were introduced by representatives of different organizational theories for the purpose of clarifying their perspectives on organizations. Later, the terms in part became used by organizational practitioners as well. The analogy of the *machine* is surely one of the oldest metaphors and is always used when the "ideal" formal structure to achieve a certain goal is defined (see Weber, 1976: 561f.). Here, one can proceed under the assumption that there is an ideal form of organization for modern society, as did the organizational researchers who followed immediately in the wake of Max Weber. Or, one can attempt to define the "optimal machine" for each respective product, technology, or client group, as practiced by the so-called contingency theorists and also the proponents of the transaction cost approach.

Distancing themselves from the associations of regularity, calculability, and plannability which the machine analogy evokes, representatives of micro-political organizational theory use the *game* metaphor to emphasize the unpredictable, unplannable and anomalous aspects of organizations (see Crozier and Friedberg, 1977: 113). The function of the *façade* for organizations receives particular emphasis by the so-called neo-institutionalists. In their opinion, organizations are primarily concerned with gaining legitimation within their environments. This explains why they create positions for gender equality, environmental protection, and efficiency officers, adapt their programs to contemporary management methods, and recruit personnel that are uniform with respect to gender, race, and class origin—or, more recently, heterogeneous in that regard, to conform with diversity, the new management buzzword—even when it makes no sense at all from an efficiency standpoint (see Meyer and Rowan, 1977: 340ff.).

Organizations have trained specialists corresponding to each of the three aspects: the machine, the game, and the façade. Middle management is dominated by specialists in the formal programming of organizations. This is where targets are conceived and new rules formulated which the employees must observe. These formal targets must then be implemented in the organization's operative areas. But this often requires much playful creativity in interpreting, reinterpreting, and dodging the formalized requirements. Understandably, the person who specializes in the informal side of things is not flagged on the organizational chart, for example, as a "Chief Informality Officer," but often it is the employees in the human resources development or the training and education departments who assume the role of contacts for everything that isn't readily subsumed under the organization's formal structure. One of the major responsibilities of those who hold top positions is to prepare the organization's external appearance, with assistance from their communications, press, and marketing departments. Sociologist Talcott Parsons (1960: 59ff.) differentiating between three basic and separate managerial functions calls this the "institutional function" of management.

In turn, such organizational specialists who in a given situation primarily manage one specific aspect of the organization fall back on external service providers. For the formal structure, the McKinseys and PricewaterhouseCoopers of the world are called in. They are expected to re-engineer the organization's formal processes, make the organizational chart leaner by dismantling departments or hierarchies, or redesign the formal classification of employees. Since such reorganization causes disruption, "cultural specialists" from outside are brought on board in the form of process consultants, trainers, and coaches whose task it is to ensure that the chemistry—the informal arrangements reached outside the scope of the formal parameters—between members is right again. When it comes to external appearances, marketing specialists, advertising companies, and PR agencies are hired to construct, tend, and, if necessary, repair the organization's façade.

This type of focus on a single individual aspect of the organization is supported by the manner in which training programs, university curricula, and continuing education courses convey knowledge about organizations. Classical education in business economics focuses on the formal aspects. Granted, the modules "Organizations I" and "Organizations II" drum various forms of organizations into the minds of students, for example, the line organization, the divisional organization, and the matrix organization. But informality is frequently treated merely as a manifestation of organizational culture. The ability to capture informal processes systematically is not imparted. Then, organizational psychology, business and industrial sociology, or organizational anthropology step in and claim that the informal processes of an organization, its cultural and underlife fall under their purview. Interesting though their observations may be, they frequently do not establish sufficiently strong linkages between the functioning of the organization's formal aspect and its exterior display. Knowledge about the construction, maintenance, and repair of an organization's façade is imparted primarily through academic coursework in communications, design, or media studies. It is rather rare for this process to convey a deeper understanding, one that has been informed by organizational research, of the way the façade interacts with an organization's informal aspects.

Taking a Look at the Interactions between the Three Aspects

Naturally, experts consider it good style to emphasize that although their specialty and focus lies in one aspect of an organization, they always keep an eye on the other angles as well. The specialists who focus on revamping the organization's formal structure by redrawing the organizational chart, optimizing programs, and conducting mergers with other organizations emphasize that one obviously cannot change an organization without giving due consideration to its culture. They therefore recommend a concomitant "cultural program." And the organizational culture specialists, the informality experts, underscore that their programs can be conducted only after they have gained a precise understanding of both the organization's façade and its formal aspects. Finally, the façade specialists stress that it is part of their professional approach never to design the external face of an organization without establishing close links to the formal and informal structures within.

Ultimately, however, the experts tend to think of their own perspective in terms of absolutes. The experts in formal structure frequently view the widely diverse forms of informality in an organization and the everyday infractions of the rules from one perspective only: this has to be "fixed." The next step is to call in quality management consultants who are charged with identifying frequent deviations from the rules and eliminating them. Comprehensive organizational management software is purchased as a means of making technical provisions against deviations from standards. Or, specific departments are set up to control processes or ensuring conformity, which is currently known as "compliance." Here, the goal is to keep deviations from the rules to a minimum. Finally, the culture experts often view the informal work processes as both a "stronghold of humaneness" in an alienated working environment as well as the "key to increased profitability." Thus, improving the organization's chemistry is seen as a launching point for creating happier employees as well as increasing the bottom line. At the highest management echelons, one notices that there is a preference for viewing internal processes from the perspective of the organization's external appearance. As early as 1938, Chester Barnard (1938: 120), who held a top-level position at the telecommunications company AT&T for a time, noted that senior executives frequently cannot keep track of their own organization's rules and regulations and are to no small degree clueless as to the factors, attitudes and behaviors that shape the organization from day to day.

Specializing and focusing on one particular aspect of an organization makes sense in terms of the division of labor. Just as it makes sense for companies to employ specialists in the fields of purchasing, production, and sales, or for a hospital to employ separate experts to provide medical care, handle the accounting for services performed, and to clean the corridors, it also appears to make functional sense that organizations keep people with different kinds of expertise on hand to manage their formal structures, their informal aspects, and their façades. A cabinet minister would be expecting too much of herself, not to mention her ministry, if—in addition to functioning as a display window for political decisions—she also aspired to understanding the relevant formal rules and regulations that applied to the organization and to keeping track of the various informal coordination processes within her ministry. For a production line worker in a fish-packing factory, it is sufficient if she is instructed which formal demands apply to her and learns how to circumvent them informally if the need should arise. She does not need to feel responsible for the construction of the company's external image.

In the analysis of organizations, my suggestion—and this may sound demanding—is to distinguish systematically between all three aspects. Even the majority of organizational theorists work only with a single differentiation—if they differentiate at all—between the formal aspect, which is suitable for presenting the organization to the external world, and an informal side, which is better withheld from public view. Yet if the goal is to gain a comprehensive understanding of the way an organization works, one must not only be able to grasp all three aspects and their respective logics, but also to understand how those three factors intermesh.

THE FORMAL ASPECT: DISTRIBUTING THE BURDENS OF PROOF

One can learn a relatively large amount about an organization by observing new members as they take their first steps after joining. It makes no difference whether it's a vacation job in a company that produces washing machines, a first full-time position in a law office after completing a training program or graduating from college, or the acceptance of a senior level position in a hospital. The person is issued an ID card, receives a brief orientation to his workspace, makes the acquaintance of colleagues, is introduced to his future manager and, if necessary, introduces himself to his subordinates. Since the contract outlines the future responsibilities of the position only in broad strokes, the organization's expectations of the position are discussed in concrete terms. The newcomer receives a manual describing the operational procedures or is referred to a colleague who is in a position to explain the applicable processes.

To use the analogy of a machine, the neophyte strives to understand how the machine works, which wheel in the machinery he represents, and how it interacts with the others in the wheelwork. To put it in different terms, he acquaints himself with the organization's formal structure. But what exactly constitutes the structures of an organization? And precisely what is formal about them?

The Formal Structures of an Organization

As a concept, structure is elusive. A politician who speaks of reforming the "tax structure" would like to say that something fundamental has to change, but is trying to avoid stating how the future tax load on citizens will be reduced—if at all. When the police take action against members of a revolutionary group, protesters react with cries of discrimination against "leftist structures," but nobody takes the trouble to explain who or what is actually the object of such discrimination. Basketball coaches wholeheartedly proclaim that their central goal is to "create structures to ensure that the club's likelihood of success increases in the future," while leaving us in the dark as to exactly what they plan to change.

Thus, the concept of structure seems well suited as a means of exploiting intellectual loopholes. It is frequently used when a more precise concept doesn't exist, or when people are too lazy to find one. We have some notion of what is implied by the term *organizational structures*, namely, the relatively lasting patterns of order within organizations and the mechanisms that are used to create them "over the long term." While it seems difficult to cast the concept of structure in precise terms, the definition is simple.

Structure

There is one kind of decision made in organizations that appears to arouse particular interest, namely, those that will influence decision making in the future. Employees engage in heated discussions over which departments of the company should be merged, because they are certain that it will have ramifications for their jobs during the years ahead. The members of a political party follow the election of a new national chairperson with great interest because they realize that the outcome will affect the way the party positions itself in the future. University students sense that the passage of new examination regulations is more important than the determination of the seminar offerings for the coming semester, because the regulations create the framework within which the instructors will decide the students' failure or success.

This initial approach to a specific type of decision already puts us in a position to determine what organizational structures are. According to Herbert A. Simon, they are decisions that serve as the premises— as preconditions—for other decisions in the organization (see Simon, 1957: 34ff.). Therefore, organizational structures always involve decisions that do not exhaust themselves in a single event, but instead exert a formative influence on an array of future decisions. The decision of a technical service employee to repair a sophisticated piece of machinery on the shop floor would not yet qualify as a decision premise, because it applies only to this particular event. However, when the CEO decides that within ten minutes after a machine goes down a member of the technical service crew must be on site in the production area, a decision premise does come into play (see Luhmann, 2005a: 93ff.).

The Formal Aspect

Naturally, structures are not only present in organizations. The traffic law that requires us to drive on the right (or left) side of the road is every bit as much a structure as the understanding in a shared apartment that the bathroom has to be cleaned every week, or the agreement reached within a family that one of the marriage partners will sell his or her labor on the market at the highest possible price, while the other takes care of raising the children. Ordered social relations cannot exist unless there are some expectations as to what will happen.

The important and distinctive feature of organizations is that they can use decisions to impose conditions on their members, namely, the condition of accepting the organization's expectations structure. Specifications define from when and until when employees must be present at an organization's location, the type of work they must perform during the time they spend there, which of the other members they must heed, and whom they can ignore. A person who is not willing to comply with these expectations cannot remain a member.

Simply put, these communicated terms of membership constitute an organization's *formal structure*. They are used to determine which programs must be accepted, for example, in the form of objectives or procedures. They determine which communication channels must be accepted, for example, the extent of one's authority over coworkers or one's own duty to report to colleagues. And they stipulate that one must accept as communication partners a wide range of individuals with whom one would not spend a moment of one's personal time.

In order to turn a certain behavior into a condition of membership, it is necessary to keep the organization's demands on its employees relatively consistent. If a formal regulation requires that a social worker takes support measures only if a client can present written proof of eligibility, while there is a simultaneous requirement that he provides immediate assistance in cases of severe neglect, then establishing that the social worker has broken the rules will pose a problem.

It is only because the formal structure of organizations demands consistency that the metaphor of a *machine* can be applied. The organization's formal expectations must be synchronized and not fundamentally contradict one another. As a result, the organization's routines, dependability, and efficiency make it appear to function like a machine in the eyes of those whose focus is fixed on formal structure.

Naturally, every organization has its inconsistent rules. But these very contradictions in the formal regulations have a tendency to alleviate the burdensome behavioral expectations on members, because in each respective case they allow the members to cite the rule that suits them (see Luhmann, 1964: 155). Consequently, when inconsistencies in the rules surface, an organization's reflex reaction is generally to "fix that." If it becomes known that state regulations are inconsistent with respect to politicians' personal use of government vehicles, it takes no more than the exposure of a single case of improper use to generate pressure that the regulations be clarified. The efforts of organizations to flag behaviors as conditions of membership apparently have the effect of keeping the rules and regulations at least somewhat consistent.

The Formal Structures

The members of organizations need a rule that enables them to identify the organization's membership expectations, which is to say, its formal structure. To that end, members check to see whether the expectations placed on them have been codified in the form of an organizational "decision" or not. A teacher will examine which decisions have been reached—for example, in the form of curricula—with respect to designing teaching plans for her classes. A person who is employed at the revenue office will investigate whether there has been a decision affecting the dates that sales taxes must be declared.

Succinctly put, one might refer to an organization's formal structures as the "decided decision premises." And even though this definition may seem somewhat awkward at first glance, it offers the advantage of immediately opening a perspective on a range of different aspects. The definition sharpens our perception of the various types of decision premises organizations can use to influence decisions, and it quickly leads to the realization that there are different ways of reaching decided decision premises, depending on whether they are governed by majority vote, consensus, or by order from on high. Not least, the definition opens our eyes to the fact that undecided decision premises may form inside organizations.

The Function of Formal Structure

Initially, decision premises represent restrictions. The regulation of business hours limits the time when communications, record keeping, governing, or marching are allowed to take place in the organization. A hierarchy of positions determines who has official permission to talk to whom, and who doesn't. The formally defined division of labor determines who is required to perform certain duties and—of particular interest—who is not required to and wouldn't be allowed to even if he so desired.

Why do organizations go to so much trouble in the first place? Why do they form their own structures?

Relieving the Need for Review

Structures are preconditions that no longer need to be scrutinized when they are applied (see Luhmann, 2003: 31ff.). If a research budget of $1 million has been approved, the person in charge of disbursing the funds does not need to—and, indeed, *should not*—conduct a review of whether the money might be better spent on nature conservation. Thus, structures not only make it unnecessary to question decisions, they actually discourage it. This is exactly what is meant by the concept of a *premise*.

That doesn't mean that an organization's every premise has to be contentious. The hiring of a new trainer for a professional sports team may have been heatedly discussed in the boardroom and may not have enjoyed support from the fan base. Yet it cannot and must not be second-guessed when each individual decision is made. Criticizing the structure of an organization—if undertaken at all—is left to specialists or restricted to very brief periods of time.

This process allows decision premises to significantly relieve pressure at all levels. Employees at the implementation level only need to consider whether their decisions match the organization's formal framework, and no longer need to examine why the rules were adopted, which alternatives exist, or which arguments could be fielded against them. Employees in executive positions, meanwhile, are safe in the assumption that the decisions made at the implementation level conform to the formal objectives and that no resource-intensive examinations of their rationality are taking place there.

This can be easily verified through a crisis experiment. As a member of an organization, all one has to do is take seriously the claims advanced in any number of management advice books and, instead of blindly performing the actions one is expected to perform, challenge them in every instance on principle. This would entail questioning the rationality of every hand movement on a company production line, reviewing a government agency's every file, or every new application for a developmental aid project. All instructions from above would be reviewed to ensure that one's manager has not only the organizational authority to issue them but also the requisite professional competence. Most organizations would be ruined by the complexity this would generate.

The prominent concepts of *uncertainty absorption* (see March and Simon, 1958: 158) and *complexity reduction* (see Luhmann, 1973a: 182ff.) serve to describe the alleviating effect that structures produce. In view of the multitude of possible alternative decisions, it is the decision premises that contribute to absorbing basic uncertainty about reaching the correct decision and reducing organizational complexity, that is, the number of available options.

Allocating the Burden of Proof

Nevertheless, organizational structures—as the premises of future decisions—do not *determine* the precise manner in which decisions are made. Even in highly standardized work processes such as a production line, a call center, or a marching formation, it is impossible to determine every single decision. Research in organizational psychology has documented that even production line workers, call-center employees, and marching soldiers frequently deviate from their strictly programmed activities (see the impressive research by Burawoy, 1979: 71ff.).Therefore, an organization's structures can provide no ultimate certainty regarding the decisions that its members will make.

But if decision premises do not determine each individual decision, then what function *do* they have?

In brief, organizational structures, that is, decision premises, distribute the burdens of proof. If one acts in accordance with the formal structure, one can do so without attracting attention, causing commotion, or being forced to justify oneself. Members of the organization then have no need to further legitimize their actions by arguing their rationality. Instead, it is sufficient if the individual points out that his actions are in conformity with the program. When they are bombing an enemy, soldiers can stay on the safe side by following army procedures and carrying out the orders of their superiors.

In addition, an organization's members always have the option of reaching a decision that runs counter to an orientation based on the premises. However, when they do so, they then bear the burden of proof. If they ignore proper channels and cut across departmental boundaries in their communications, when a conflict arises they will have to justify their reasons for taking the shortcut. A person caught performing a work process in an effective albeit formally prohibited manner, should have good evidence that the procedure in question only benefits the organization and does not create any identifiable damage. One must hope that acting in such a way will be deemed useful to the organization and either silently tolerated or, in the event of a dispute, recognized as advantageous (see Dalton, 1959: 237).

What emerges is that organizational structures merely make certain decisions more likely than others. Organizational sociologist Erhard Friedberg points out that they do not directly determine the actions of the organization's members but rather define their "latitude to negotiate" (see Friedberg, 1993: 151). To use the language of institutional economics, structures form a network of contracts, although the players can never be certain that the other side will truly comply (see Reve, 1990: 133ff.). Structures direct actions along certain pathways; they make some decisions subject to accountability, while exempting others. A systems theorist would say that structures encourage some communications while discouraging others.

It is only because decision premises function in this way that organizations can operate securely in a field defined by the tension between simultaneous demands for both stability and flexibility. Because of the way the burden of proof is allocated, fundamental change welling up from below tends to be unlikely: all deviation entails the danger of being forced to justify itself. Yet at the same time, deviations that are functional for the organization may evolve and thereby soften the rigidity of formal structures that have been decreed from above.

The Types of Formal Structures: Programs, Communication, and Personnel

We can agree relatively quickly on the elements that constitute an organization's formal structure. Depending on the type of organization, one would include the organizational chart, work processes, working-time regulations, managerial planning systems, directives, organizational manuals, procedures, computer software, bylaws, hierarchical ranks, business policies, sign-off policies, and operating instructions.

But how can this array of diverse elements be ordered so that it can be used to gain insight into the way an organization functions? Should we differentiate between three "hard elements" (strategy, structure, and system) and four "soft elements" (shared values, skills, style, staff), call it a "7S model," and then proclaim the interplay between the factors as a recipe for all organizational success, as management consultants Tom Peters and Robert Waterman attempted (1982: 32)? Should we follow organizational scientist Henry Mintzberg (1979: 19ff.) and differentiate between five areas of an organization, namely, a "strategic apex," an "operating core," a "middle line," a "technostructure," and "support staff," and then analyze how they interact? Or should we use the approach proposed by economist Fritz Nordsieck (1932) and simply distinguish between "structural organizations" and "process organization?"

Distinguishing between three different types of structures has proved to be a successful approach. The first type are the *decision programs*. Management planning programs, directives, computer software, and business policies fall into this category. They are used to determine which actions in the organization are to be viewed as right, and which as wrong. The second type of structure consists of *communication channels*. These include the rules and procedures, the division of labor, the flow of information, co-signing authority, the hierarchical structure, or rules concerning signatures. Here, the purpose is to define the manner in which information can and must be communicated within the organization and the pathways it must follow. *Personnel* can be viewed as the third type of structure or decision premise. Here, the underlying consideration is that the individual (or the type of individual) who is placed in a given position will make a difference for future decisions (see Luhmann, 2005a: 93ff.; for a detailed examination see Luhmann, 2000: 221ff.).

Programs

Programs bundle the criteria that must be used in reaching decisions. They determine which actions are permitted, and which are not. In that respect, programs have the function of allowing the attribution of accountability when errors are made, and thereby distributing accusations in the organization. If an employee does not meet the goal of increasing revenues by ten percent, as specified by the program, she may try to find excuses, but ultimately the program allows the fault to be sought primarily with her. In principle, there are two different kinds of programs: conditional programs and goal programs (see Luhmann, 1976: 104).

Conditional programs determine which actions must be taken when an organization registers a certain impulse. For example, if a pre-assembled component arrives at a workstation on an assembly line, then, according to a company-determined conditional program, a certain action must be undertaken. If an application for unemployment benefits is received by an unemployment office, the caseworker can use conditional programs that are specified by the agency and essentially regulated by law to determine precisely whether or not the circumstances warrant the payment of support (see Luhmann, 1982c: 174ff).

Consequently, in conditional programs there is a strong link between the prerequisite for an action, the *if*, and the execution of a decision, the *then*. The procedure is precisely defined. The program determines what must be done, and, in the case of conditional programs, what is not expressly permitted is forbidden. For an employee whose job is subject solely to conditional programs, discretionary power is at best limited.

The attribution of responsibility for errors functions analogously. If a person who is performing an action registers an impulse and does not take the prescribed measures, he has committed an error and can be held accountable. Conversely, if the person performing the task follows the program correctly, it is not he who bears the responsibility for the outcome of the process, but rather the person who developed the program. For example, if a social worker handles her caseload in accordance with the prescribed conditional programs, she cannot be faulted if, in the end, a homeless person dies on the streets of London. Rather, responsibility lies with those in the administration who set up the conditional programs in such a way that the death could not be prevented.

Conditional programs are therefore *input oriented*. The person who performs the task receives an input in the form of an application, a criminal complaint, or movement on a conveyor belt, and this triggers a prescribed sequence of work steps. As a result, organizational processes that are governed by conditional programs are well predictable, but they lack flexibility and outcome sensitivity.

Goal programs are entirely different from conditional programs in the way they are constructed. Goal programs determine which targets or objectives are to be achieved. Goal programming is found at the top of an organization, for example, when a company sets the goal of achieving the leadership position in the washing machine market. However, goal programming also takes place in the activities of middle and lower management when the so-called "management by objectives" approach is taken. But even simple activities can be governed by goal programs, for example, when a manager asks her assistant to buy 2,000 sheets of printer paper at the best possible price.

In goal programs, the choice of means is left open. The object is to reach the stated goal, no matter how. Granted, the choice of means must remain within certain boundaries which have been established by the rules of the organization or even by legal statute. The CEO's assistant may not simply steal the paper from the department next door and then point out that she had chosen the cheapest alternative. Nevertheless, as a rule of thumb all means that are not prohibited by the organization (or by law) are permissible if they serve to achieve the goal.

When goal programs are involved, the person who implements the program bears the responsibility if the goal or the objective is not achieved, or if the means to achieve the objective creates problematic side effects for the organization. The assistant will be hard pressed for an explanation if the printer paper does not materialize, or even if obtaining the paper entails too much effort. She can try to find excuses, for example, by pointing to the intrinsic logic of an SAP-driven purchasing system, but even such attempts at justification indicate that the error is initially being attributed to her.

Since goal programs are *output oriented*, they can be geared to an indeterminable point in the future. Requiring the assistant to always make certain that there is enough printer paper available ensures that supplies will be maintained regardless of whether paper usage in the immediate future fluctuates widely either up or down. Goal programming thereby allows the organization to acquire a certain elasticity which it would not achieve through conditional programming alone.

Communication Channels

Communication channels account for the second basic type of organizational decision premises. Initially, establishing legitimate points of contact, proper channels, and domains of responsibility massively limits the opportunities for communication. In reaching its decisions, the organization dispenses with a large number of possible contacts as well as the participation of the entire range of potentially helpful and interested players. Only a limited number of legitimized contacts and authorized decision makers are permitted, which the members must respect if they do not wish to jeopardize their membership. Defining such communication channels is an organization's only means of preventing communications overkill. Other social formations such as families, groups, or conversations may well organize themselves as all-channel-networks where every member of the family, every participant in the conversation, or every member of the group can communicate with every other member and, at least in principle, demand to have a voice in important questions. In organizations, it is precisely this possibility that the determination of communication channels precludes.

For the members of an organization, defined communication channels have an unburdening effect, as do all of the other types of structure. Those who are responsible for a certain decision may assume that the matter is considered correct within the system and will not be questioned. On the other hand, if a problem arises they must also assume responsibility and account for potential errors or the negative consequences of their decisions. This not only takes the onus off their superiors who can assume that subordinates will follow their instructions, or at least officially act as if they were. It also takes the onus off the subordinates, because they know with whom they may and may not speak. Well-defined communication channels also relieve cooperative efforts between two people at the same level, for example, because one department does not have to verify the correctness or usefulness of information received from another.

There is a wide variety of ways to regulate communications within an organization.

The most prominent method of putting firm communication channels in place is certainly through a *hierarchy*. On the one hand, hierarchies define who is subordinate or superior to whom and therefore establish inequality. Yet at the same time they also produce equality because they specify which departments are situated on the same hierarchical level. The central function of hierarchies is, as has been shown, to allow the rapid resolution of work-related conflict by referencing the terms of membership.

A further important method of establishing communication channels is *co-signing authority* which is generally set up on the same hierarchical level. A number of different government ministers must agree before a statute can become effective; or, the department heads have to countersign work instructions before they can be officially announced in the organization. Co-signing authority is based on the equality of rank among the participating organizational units. It is therefore correspondingly sensitive because there are no simple solutions when conflicts arise.

Another, increasingly important way of defining communication channels is to view them in terms of *project structures*. To this end, members of different departments are assembled to work on a project—which is to say, a goal program—over a specific period of time. Frequently in such cases, the project leaders are invested with either limited authority or none at all. Meanwhile, the participants in the project often retain a sense of duty toward the branch of the hierarchy that dispatched them. This, in turn, weakens the additional communication pathway that arose through the project group itself.

Hierarchies, co-signing authority, and project structures can be combined with one another to produce their own highly specific forms and networks of communication channels. Depending on the combination of hierarchies, co-signing authority, and project structures elected, there will be a corresponding change in the likelihood of cooperation, competition, or conflict in the organization. Organizational science mobilizes a high degree of creativity to develop, name, and describe such networked communication channels. Concepts such as a functional organization, divisional organization, or matrix organization are then used to articulate the dominant organizing principle that underlies them.

Personnel

Whereas it is common practice in organizational science to classify programs and communication channels as organizational structures, the suggestion to view personnel as a third and coequal type of structure is somewhat surprising. The reason that personnel has been widely ignored in this context can be found in a blind spot that crept into organizational research via classical economics. Due to its orientation on the classic goal-means model, managerial organizational research often views personnel merely as a means to an end, but not as something that represents a structure. This erroneous conclusion leads to the use of such peculiar terminological hybrids as "organization and personnel" in the names of departments, institutes, or academic chairs—suggesting that in analytical terms personnel is somehow positioned outside of the organization (Luhmann, 1971c: 209).

Using the concept of organizational structures as explained above, however, it is easy to document the structural character of personnel-related decisions. It will be clear to any observer that the matter entails more than an organization reaching decisions *about* personnel;

personnel decisions also represent important premises for further decisions in the organization. In terms of future decisions, it makes a difference who occupies the position responsible for making them. Given the same position, a lawyer will often reach different decisions to an economist, who, in turn, will arrive at different decisions to a sociologist. People with upper-class socialization tend to reach different decisions to those from the lower social strata. It is also said that decision behavior in women tends to differ from men.

The importance of this structural type can also be gauged by the fact that organizations take a keen interest in people. Despite all the gossip about alleged affairs between board members and their fitness trainers, the primary issue here is not that people are found interesting in a personal sense. Rather, this pronounced interest in people is based on the assumption that each individual will reach decisions in his or her own specific manner. One can observe that the members of an organization develop their own style with respect to their manner of implementing programs and using communication channels (see Jackall, 1983: 121). And one realizes that every personnel change creates discontinuity, even if the organization's communication channels and programs remain identical.

Organizations have different options when it comes to turning the personnel adjustment screw (Luhmann, 1971c: 208). The *hiring process* determines which type of person will make future decisions. Even the wording of job advertisements, candidate profiles, and position requirements often involves heated debate over the qualities a person should possess—and which will ultimately translate into a decision-making style that has bearing on the organization.

The *firing* of individuals can be used to signal the kind of decisions the organization no longer wishes to have in the future. Particularly at the highest levels, this option is frequently used to send an internal and external message that different forms of decisions are expected. Yet there are many positions where termination is not an option. Here, many times the only alternative is to resort to a transfer, in other words, to move the individuals to positions where their decisions "can't do so much damage."

Internal transfers can be made in several directions: upward—in the form of a promotion, or to put someone on ice as a figurehead; downward—in the form of a demotion; or lateral. Transfers offer the advantage that the person is already known in the organization and can be assessed, although the performance that was valued in one position does not guarantee that the person will perform correspondingly well in other capacities. Conversely, failure in one position doesn't imply that the person is unsuited for other jobs as well.

Personnel development represents an attempt at changing people's behavior, so that while remaining in the same position they will reach different decisions in the future. Here, one often has the impression that personnel represents the organization's software, so to speak, and can be re-programmed in any way one desires through coaching and training seminars. In contrast, the organization's programs, technologies, and official procedures constitute its hardware. Yet the opposite seems to be more plausible. Whereas an organization's plans and task descriptions can be "easily changed, practically with the stroke of a pen," people "can only be changed with difficulty, if at all" (Luhmann, 2000: 280). Even if individuals are willing to change as a result of personnel development measures, their work environment often confronts them with the expectation that they should behave the same way they always have.

On the Relationship Between Programs, Communication Channels, and Personnel

The interaction of programs, communication channels, and personnel can be observed even in the smallest unit that can be defined in an organizational sense, namely, a *position*. A position must be occupied by a person. A position is programmed either by trigger conditions (conditional programs) that are determined through organizational operating manuals or computer programs, or by targets that must be met (goal programs); its contact options are restricted by existing communication channels (see Luhmann, 1973b). But the *departments* of an organization are also places where all three types of structure always act in concert. A department is shaped by its personnel and their often highly individual decision-making styles. The department's work is structured through goal and conditional programs as well as through its integration into the organization's communication channels. Finally, the interaction of the three forms of structure can also be observed at the level of the *organization* overall, for example, when it becomes apparent that a company always hires one certain type of employee, when one notices that a change in the corporate chart is opening up entirely new and unaccustomed communication channels, or when one observes organization-wide changes occurring in goals or procedures.

What To Do? Approaches to the Analysis and Modification of Organizational Structures

Initially, breaking down an organization's formal structure into the three types of decision structures discussed above seems to be a finger exercise that offers little satisfaction. It creates additional analytical concepts but does not provide any decision recommendations for the organization itself. In contrast, examining the interaction of programs, communication channels, and personnel puts us in a position to ask questions that focus attention not only on an organization's potential for change but also on the limitations of such change.

Which Types of Structure are Created During Growth?

During their founding stages, organizations are generally reluctant to form well-defined structures, that is, decision premises. They often dispense with definitive programming for their processes because standardization is not yet viewed as a necessity, and the members are developing routines through learning-by-doing. Along the same lines, they often do without formally prescribed communication channels. Each member can approach every other member more or less without difficulty, which is why these organizations can also be called face-to-face organizations. Yet this imbues the *personnel* decision premise with a central importance that can be seen, among other things, in the repeated emphasis (particularly in early-stage organizations) on the fact that the chemistry between the founding members has to be right—and in the momentous effect that the departure of individual members frequently has on the organization.

Nevertheless, relatively soon after the organizations have been founded, tried and true practices evolve, and communications begin to follow well-trodden paths. But the practices and pathways are supported only by daily routines, and consequently, if a deviation occurs, one's ability to protest is at best limited. As the organization continues to grow, these decision premises—which were never truly brought to a decision—are successively codified, altered, or even banned through official decisions.

Following the founding stage, one can observe the way start-up companies, new government agencies, alternative media projects, or political initiatives that at one time reached their decisions by and large without the support of premises, begin to invest increasing amounts of energy in finding stability through structures by specifying binding goals, creating standardized processes, establishing hierarchies and allocating co-signing authority, and introducing official personnel policies. It is interesting to observe the degree to which stability is sought by finalizing programs or formalizing communication channels, and the degree to which the decision premise personnel continues to play a role.

Which Types of Structure Have Been Immobilized?

Examining the different forms of organizational structures allows us to recognize which structural elements are immobile, that is, they can only be changed at the cost of losing identity or cannot be changed at all. To illustrate, in Protestant churches, Islamic religious communities, and Jewish congregations it can be observed that an important component of the *program*, namely, reference to the Old and New Testaments, the Koran, or the Talmud, is treated as sacrosanct and has therefore been immobilized as a decision premise. An immobilization of programs also took place in Marxist-Leninist party organizations under state socialism through the dogmatization of the writings of Karl Marx and Friedrich Engels. As a result of these constellations, changes can only be undertaken if deference is shown to the immobilized decision premises. If the books of Matthew, Mark, Luke, and John, or the works of Marx and Engels, are taken as absolutes, the only possible program flexibility lies in the interpretation of programs and in the guidelines for executing them (see Luhmann, 2003: 175f.).

An organization's *communication channels* can also be immobilized. For example, political parties in democratic countries are not only participants in a macro-democratic game, they themselves must also act as if their communication channels were democratic. Even if successful politics, as Max Weber remarked (1919: 39f.), consists of turning party members into "well-disciplined voting fodder," and the party is essentially governed by its own oligarchy, the formal communication channels must present themselves in a different way, namely, as those of an organization which is governed from below, and where all important questions are ultimately decided by the party base. In many countries, an attempt to transform these communication channels along the lines of dictatorial leadership would run afoul of the constitution and result in the prohibition of the party.

In many cases, the structural characteristic of the *personnel* is also immobilized. One sees particularly striking cases of this in family-held companies, where there is a preference for recruiting leadership personnel from the family of the principals. This severely curtails flexibility in personnel selection. Granted, one can choose between various members of the family, for example, between the first-born and the second-born daughter, one can allow individual family members to grow into positions slowly, and also transfer ill-suited family members to somewhat less important positions. Yet filling positions from the outside is generally avoided because the character of the family enterprise would be lost.

In Which Respects Can the Types of Structure Replace One Another?

The types of organizational structures can also be viewed under the aspect of their mutual replaceability. When a task—say, the development of a new medication, or victory in battle, or school reform—cannot be programmed in detail, the demands placed on the person making the decisions increase almost automatically. Or, conversely, if a person does not possess all of the necessary abilities, then either the involvement of other positions must be ordered, hierarchical supervision intensified, or the program screw tightened. If it is impossible to rely on either the programs or the personnel, then the organization must rely on its communication channels in the form of a deeply layered hierarchy, as seen in low-wage factories in China or Mexico (see Luhmann, 2000: 226).

This type of replacement of structural characteristics can be observed in all reform processes. The modularization and standardization of academic courses of study at universities tends to result in a loss of importance for the personnel decision premise. The content and form of examinations and, with some limitations, also the form and content of instruction become so standardized that the question of who teaches the course or conducts the examinations becomes secondary. In extreme cases, study guides are distributed, ready-made PowerPoint presentations are projected onto the wall, and standard tests are drawn up. Thus, due to the precision programming, the person who conducts the course is no longer a matter of primary concern. The knowledge that the students have acquired is evaluated using multiple choice tests which can ultimately be graded by student assistants or the secretary, or even fed directly into a computer.

THE INFORMAL ASPECT: EXCHANGE AND BULLYING IN ORGANIZATIONS

As a newcomer in an organization, one recognizes relatively quickly that getting ahead takes more than merely adhering to the formal structures. Even during the first few days on the job, one is confronted with expectations that were neither outlined beforehand in the job description, specified in process manuals, nor articulated as direct instructions from one's manager.

In the run-up to joining an organization, only the formal expectations can be put into words, for example, who the new employee will report to and which of the official regulations will apply to her. All of these matters can be arranged through formal decisions. By contrast, integration into the organization's informal structure cannot be settled conclusively. Requirements of that kind could be rejected as inappropriate by the prospective employee because the organization itself often doesn't recognize its own informal structures, and even if it did, it wouldn't be permissible to condone them officially. It is difficult to make it clear to a new employee that her main task will consist of cushioning her colleagues from their top-level manager and her occasional outbreaks of rage. A new field representative in the pharmaceutical industry can only receive the most indirect kind of information about the methods the company uses (and which may border on illegality) to influence a doctor's prescribing habits in favor of a certain medication.

Nevertheless, experience generally shows that members of organizations fail if they adhere too closely, or exclusively, to formal demands. The world of an organization seems a much wilder place than is conveyed through its well-communicated formal structure or even the external façade it presents to non-members. Organizational research applies a range of different terms to this "wild life." One speaks of "informality" as distinct from formality (see Barnard, 1938: 120); of an organization's "underlife" which forms beyond the reach of the official regulations (see Goffman, 1973: 169ff.); or of "organizational culture" which significantly shapes an organization's actions (see Pettigrew, 1979: 570ff.).

But what does it really mean? What constitutes informality in an organization? How does an underlife transpire? What accounts for the culture of an organization?

The Informal Structures

Informality is often understood, and misunderstood, as a "stronghold of human kindness" or as the precinct of "humane relationships" within the hard steel shell of an organization. According to this view, it is here that "people can still be human beings," while in other respects the organization has been shaped by "conditions of capitalist exploitation," "bureaucratic administrative ideologies," or "alienated work activities." It is asserted that informality allows emotional, playful interactions to develop between people, whereas they are otherwise required to function like gears in a machine.

Yet it is misleading to attempt to give the definition of informality a humanistic tint. The initiation rites that boarding schools, military units, or university fraternities use to admit newcomers into the organization also in an informal sense cannot always be reconciled with the UN Charter for Human Rights. The methods that cliques in organizations use to achieve their expectations are often more brutal than the means superiors have at their disposal to crack down, because superiors are restricted to the formal structure. Instead of viewing informality in terms that are charged with positive moral connotations, we must first define precisely what we mean by informality in contrast to formal structure.

The Structures

A single deviation from the rule, a single occurrence of an unaccustomed procedure would not cause us to speak of informality, or of an organization's culture or underlife; we speak in those terms only when we recognize that the deviation occurs with a certain regularity, one might say, when it has a structural quality. It is not when a pattern is used by a single individual alone, but rather when it has crept into and can be now be expected in parts of the organization as such, that it achieves the status of an informally proven mode of thinking and acting. It is only when a last-minute arrangement with a colleague in a neighboring department does not represent an exception but is repeatedly used to "cut the red tape" that one is dealing with an informal structure. Thus, informality is not defined as a one-time improvisation used to clear a swath through the jungle of requirements and regulations, but rather a network of reliable organizational pathways that are traveled time and time again.

There is an easy way to recognize whether an informal structure is involved or merely a one-time deviation: the reaction of others. If they are expecting a behavior, even if it entails an infraction against the organization's formal regulations, or actually involves breaking the law, then it is a matter of structure. Whereas, if the other members are confused, react with uncertainty, or become angry, one can be sure that one's own behavior is not covered by informal structural expectations. For example, in the game of soccer there is an unwritten law that a team will voluntarily send the ball out of bounds when a player on the opposing team is injured. If a player dares to break this rule, it is not the referee who enforces the informal expectations—after all, he is only in charge of the written regulations—but rather the whistles from the fans, "messages" which cannot be misunderstood from the opposing team, or even pressure from his own team members. In other words, in this case the dominant expectation, the structure, is to abstain from using an opportunity, as opposed to trying to exploit the advantage of outnumbering the opponent to score a goal—which would otherwise be perfectly legitimate.

Thus, informal structures are also *decision premises*, preconditions that apply to a wide range of decisions in the organization. And yet, to ask the obvious follow-up question, what distinguishes such informal decision premises from the decision premises in formal structures?

Informality

The definition is simple. All of the expectations in an organization that *are not* (or *cannot* be) formulated with reference to the terms of membership, are informal. A manager can approach her staff with an informal expectation, such as working longer hours than contractually stipulated, but if the staff fails to comply she cannot issue a reprimand. No legal counsel in any administration, no court martial in any army, no arbitration board of any political party, would win a trial if it had to admit that an employee had indeed acted correctly in a formal sense but had thereby transgressed the organization's informal expectations.

There can be various reasons for not including official formulations of expectations in the conditions of membership. The organization might lack the confidence to express a certain expectation unequivocally through a decision, because it could mean a loss of legitimation if the expectation were to become known. Perhaps the informal expectation runs counter to one of the organization's official doctrines, and as a result one can only allude to it. Perhaps some expectations are so hazy and vague that they defy being cast in concrete terms. The common element in all of these cases, however, is that *no* official decision was reached concerning the respective expectations and yet they exist in the organization nevertheless.

Informal practices can arise, first, at the level of individual groups within the organization. Then norms evolve, for example, that one should avoid doing an excessive amount of work so that one doesn't become an overachiever, while at the same time also not hurting the group through underperformance. Secondly, informal practices can also establish themselves at the level of entire departments or divisions. One need only think of the well-coordinated but illegal methods of ensuring customer loyalty which are practiced by some sales departments in pharmaceutical companies that are spread over several locations. And finally, informal expectations can form at the overall organizational level. For example, in many armies there is an expectation that a soldier who has been injured or killed should never be left behind in enemy territory, even if the soldiers involved in the rescue operation must risk their own lives.

Informal Structures Represent Undecided Decision Premises

If one combines the following two ideas, namely, the structurality of expectations and the impossibility of referencing the officially declared terms of membership, one arrives at a definition of informality that manages without making reference to humankind and human benevolence: informality, the underlife and culture of an organization, represents its "undecided decision premises" (Rodríguez, 1991: 140f.). Although this formulation may seem inaccessible at first glance, the underlying concept is straightforward. Agreements are reached about the manner in which organizations should make decisions in the future, but these agreements are not based on decisions taken by a board of directors, a party convention, or a pope. Instead, they have simply managed to creep in as customary practices. No amount of intensive searching would be able to link these accords to specific decisions, and yet they act as decision premises nevertheless.

Such "undecided decision premises" can have a significant degree of persistence for the very reason that they were never the outcome of a decision; consequently, it is also not so easy to make them disappear as the result of a decision. There are companies, public administrations, and hospitals where proven methods of acquiring business or awarding contract have persisted for decades and withstood not only official prohibition by the board of directors but also tougher legal sanctions. There have been cases of corporate mergers where the official regulations of the two organizations were standardized within the first six months, but the informal processes that had established themselves in one of the original organizations remained in place for decades (see Hofstede, 1993).

Why Does Informality Arise? Taking a Look at Functionality

An organization that was satisfied merely to have achieved employee compliance with its formal regulations would be lost. Those who doubt this should try doing nothing except what their organizations formally require of them for several days. Presumably, operations would more or less come to a halt. The effect would be growing pressure from colleagues and superiors to "take a more relaxed view of things" and not jeopardize the work flow by being "overly bureaucratic"—which is what adherence to the formal expectations is then called.

It is not without good reason that "working by the book" is one of the most effective forms of labor strike. It entails strict adherence to the official rules, even if they are not entirely (or at all) appropriate in the situation at hand, and would be silently ignored under normal circumstances. Employees recall outdated regulations that have never been formally rescinded and hamstring operations by observing them. They follow all rules and instructions to the letter, and precisely that paralyzes the organization. Their exclusive reliance on formal structures and the rigidity associated with them now pushes the organization to the brink of disintegration (see Crozier, 1963: 247ff.).

The realization that organizations cannot rely exclusively on their formal structures is almost as old as organizational science itself. Max Weber was already not only examining bureaucracies in considerable detail but also demonstrated the way bureaucratic structures compete—but can also cooperate—with existing personal networks (see Weber, 1976: 551ff.). Chester Barnard realized early on that one could only find one's way in an organization by recognizing the "invisible government" and appropriating the "informal processes" (see Barnard, 1938: 120).

Why do such decision premises develop in the first place?

It is Impossible to Formalize Everything

It is not possible to elevate every expectation in an organization to the level of a condition of membership. Any time that attitudes, positions, and cognitive styles are involved, difficulties in formulating the terms of membership seem to arise. Much like all other paradoxical demands, challenging a person to "be creative" is something that will elude programming by top management echelons. When the head of personnel development encourages his employees to represent company values as authentically as possible during training programs, it is something he can hardly reinforce through sanctions or control.

The impossibility of programming many expectations becomes particularly clear when dealing with non-members of the organization. Observations of flight stewardesses and stewards, or waitresses and waiters in restaurants, show that personnel can be strongly encouraged to interact cordially with patrons, but the expectation that their tone should come across as heartfelt resists programming. To paraphrase a play on words used by sociologist Arlie Russell Hochschild (1983), from the outside you can't "manage the heart" but only the façade that is erected for non-members, and that to a limited degree as well. Hochschild overlooks that feelings cannot be formalized, in stewardesses as little as in waiters, in prostitutes just as little as in pastors, which explains why emotions frequently can be institutionalized only as informal expectations. Social interactions between members is another area that is often amenable only to limited programming. It may be true that one can define the terms of membership in the form of one department's obligation to supply information to another, but it is difficult to formalize the expectation that members will behave in a collegial manner toward one another.

The expectations that cannot be completely translated into terms of membership can be called *undecidable decision premises*, as a subtype of undecided decision premises. This subsumes virtually everything that can be found on the wild lists published in practitioner literature where, in addition to "attitudes," "cognitive styles," and "positions," we also find the "recipe knowledge," "mutually shared basic assumptions," "orientation patterns," and "unquestioningly accepted causal attributions," that apply in organizations.

Some Things Do Not Become Formalized

Although some expectations could be formalized in principle, and compliance with them could be monitored, the organization consciously or unconsciously forgoes such formalization. As an example, employees may reach an agreement on a procedural shortcut which, in principle, could also be formalized through official instructions. Thus, the life of an organization is pervaded by shortcuts, tricks, and back channels which in theory could be translated into routines that are officially endorsed. Here, it is not a question of undecidable decision premises, but rather of *decision premises that are in essence decidable although no decision has been made.*

The development of this type of informality has to do with the fact that organizations are confronted with contradictory demands which cannot be resolved through decisions at the formal level. There can always only be *one* "consistently planned, legitimate formal order of expectations" in an organization (Luhmann, 1964: 155). Consequently, reacting to contradictory preconditions of existence requires a high degree of informality (see Luhmann, 1964: 154). In order to survive, organizations require "a large number of services that cannot be formulated as formal expectations." Management therefore, often has no option other than to tolerate or even promote illegality (Luhmann, 1964: 86).

Ultimately, this contributes to the fact that rules can persist in spite of their rigidity. From time to time, rules have to be broken in order to continue existing as rules (see Dalton, 1959: 219). It is only the balancing that members of the organization undertake in a given situation, namely, whether they should comply with the formal structures or take the indirect route, which allows organizations to adapt so quickly.

The Forms of Informality

We can observe different forms of informality. There are informal expectations that pertain to the organization's *programs*, for example, well-established, customary routines (conditional programs), or objectives that are not openly articulated (goal programs). Other informal expectations relate to *communication channels*. Here, an example would be when employees communicate with one another without interposing their respective superiors, or when an unofficial hierarchy evolves among employees who are equals in the formal sense. On the *personnel* level, expectations are formulated that cannot be referred to officially, for example, when employees are expected to utilize their personal contacts.

Alternately, forms of informality can also be differentiated according to their relationship to the organization's formal order. A crucial differentiation, which is often the assumption in the literature on organizational culture, is whether the informal expectations are compatible with the organization's formal body of rules and standards, whether they contain infractions against the formal expectations, or whether they might even go as far as also breaking laws that are beyond the organization's reach.

Informality That is Compatible with Formality

Organizations are home to a wide range of informal expectations that cannot be enforced by citing the terms of membership, although they also do not break any of an organization's official rules (see Luhmann, 1982c: 31ff.). In most companies, public administrations, and universities, the expectation that staff members will establish a "kitty" to finance refreshments for guests of the department does not run counter to official policy. Although the matter could in principle be the subject of a decision, pressure to contribute to the kitty is exerted only informally because one does not wish to elevate it to a condition of membership. Normally, the expectation that one will stand by a colleague and lend a hand with the job also doesn't contradict official membership expectations.

Informality that is compatible with an organization's formal structures fills regulatory gaps, but often it also provides an additional safeguard for formal expectations. In all the armies of this world, even in small East African and Central American nations, the military law books, service regulations, and orders of the day all contain wording that demands comradeship of the soldiers. Offenses such as stealing from a fellow soldier are classified as a breach of comradeship and punished more severely than would be the case in other organizations—and "fellowship evenings" are arranged as a means of strengthening camaraderie. Since rescuing a comrade from a death zone is hardly enforceable in terms of a condition of membership, armies effectively use informal expectations to make providing comradely assistance a requirement.

Informality That Breaks the Rules

In many manifestations of informality, the informal expectation can only be fulfilled by violating formal expectations. It has to do with minor or major deviations from the organization's official objectives, disregard of prescribed if-then programs, or bypassing a superior in order to move something ahead quickly. Niklas Luhmann speaks of "useful illegality," although this concept initially does not imply breaking the law in the narrower sense, but rather merely violating the rules and standards of the respective organization (see Luhmann, 1964: 304ff.).

Take the assembly of an automobile as an example. Due to product liability concerns, the connection of the axle to the steering system—which is still undertaken mechanically—must be certified by the signatures of the production engineer and the quality manager. Since gathering these signatures entails a time-consuming circulation procedure, it has become customary in many plants for the relevant foreman to obtain the signatures on blank forms in advance. This may violate the rules, but in many factories it has become a well-established practice that has never been the subject of an official decision, and never will, because of the problematical product liability questions.

When this rule-breaking type of informality is involved, superiors actually have to step in and sanction the member concerned if they become aware of the illegal activity. Otherwise their own behavior could be viewed as a violation. Consequently, senior members of an organization in particular are careful to act as if such deviations—which are, after all, often useful to the organization—were not coming to their attention. This allows them to shift responsibility to their subordinates in the event that the violations become known.

Informality That Breaks the Law

The situation escalates even further if the fulfillment of informal expectations also constitutes a violation of current law. Examples of this would be tampering with a trip recorder in a truck to illegally increase the driver's time behind the wheel; bridging the fuses on manufacturing machinery with wires in order to keep production running even though the equipment is damaged; overstepping official working-time regulations so that a job can still be finished on schedule; or the small favors shown to employee representatives whose actions would legally constitute a breach of trust. To the extent that such cases become known, it is not only the rules of the organization that apply but also the overarching governmental regulations.

Violations of the rules are sensitive to exposure from within. If a member of the organization, a so-called whistleblower, contacts a law enforcement agency, in the Western world there is virtually no way to prevent a subsequent police inquiry. The systematic bribery of awarding authorities, which major electronic concerns use to obtain contracts for the construction of power plants, subways, or airports, entails the risk that exposure will trigger an investigation, not only inside the organization but externally as well.

When violations of law are discovered, normally a heated battle over accountability ensues. The organization tries to personalize the infraction, in other words, to pin responsibility on a single member. By contrast, it is practicable for employees who have broken the law to attribute their own misconduct to the existence of general, informal expectations in the organization. If they succeed in demonstrating that their infractions resulted from implicit, regular, and endemic expectations on the part of their superiors, such circumstances will be viewed as extenuating. However, since the organizations likewise are attempting to escape responsibility, they will often offer incentives for the members to assume the guilt.

Imposing Informal Expectations

The challenge one encounters when establishing informal expectations, as we have shown, is that they cannot be imposed by linking them to the terms of membership. Since a business cannot officially announce that it is all right to exceed working-time guidelines if an order is particularly important, one also cannot officially punish employees if they leave the company at the close of the official workday. Since values such as collegiality and comradeship are so abstract that they frequently do not define concrete behavior in concrete situations, it is difficult to hold individual members of the organization officially responsible for breaking those norms. When conflicts arise, each member can retreat to his formal role. Withdrawing to that position, however, can entail only latent reproach; the organization cannot openly hold the failure against him (see Luhmann, 1964: 64). For this reason, highly specific forms of both positive and negative sanctioning have evolved as a means of imposing informal expectations.

The Principle of Exchange: Forms of Positive Sanctioning

Normally, the formal structure of an organization includes only a small number of exchange elements. Generally speaking, members of organizations receive flat-rate wages and cannot expect to receive additional reward or remuneration from their colleagues, superiors, or subordinates for every action they perform. When an employee does not pass information to a colleague as he is formally required to do, but instead tries to frame his provision of the information as a personal favor, his colleague will be annoyed. A secretary who expects her boss to provide more than symbolic recognition for typing each letter— pralines and flowers, special vacations, or extended work breaks—will have difficulty holding her position (see Luhmann, 1964: 288ff.).

Thus, while organizations are constructed in an "exchange-averse" manner in terms of their formal structure, exchange plays a pivotal role in imposing informal expectations. For example, an expectation evolves among miners that they will really pitch in during working hours underground and even exceed formal targets, so that after three or four days of hard work they can take a day off that is actually not scheduled and get drunk together. One concession is traded for another (Gouldner, 1954).

From the perspective of exchange processes, it can be purposeful to hopelessly overwhelm members of the organization with formal expectations, as is sometimes the case. The incessant violations of the formal expectations create opportunities for superiors to exercise sanctions which, in turn, can be exchanged for good conduct on the part of their subordinates. Research conducted on armies shows that soldiers find themselves "trapped by norms." A multitude of formal regulations ranging from proper physical posture and the correct way to salute, to personal hygiene, the care of uniforms, and the cleanliness of their quarters and equipment puts them in a position where they are constantly vulnerable to criticism (see Treiber, 1973: 51). This enables superiors to create goodwill in their subordinates by tolerating their violations of formal expectations. In turn, the goodwill can be used to impose behaviors on the subordinates which are not covered by the formal structure. Yet in some cases subordinates can also profit from the fact that their organization is strictly formalized. Elaborate regulations, accurate instructions, bureaucratic specifications, and precisely defined working hours represent more for employees than just restrictions. Rather, according to sociologist Alvin W. Gouldner (1954), they can always be used as bargaining chips vis-à-vis superiors when deviations from the rules become necessary.

Such exchange relationships are rarely discussed openly. An outspoken deal such as, "You will now allow me to smoke in my office, and in return I'll stay later today" is more often the exception. Instead, the assumption is that the pay-off for an informal concession made to a colleague, a superior, or a subordinate will materialize later (see Luhmann, 2002: 44). Members pave the unofficial pathways with favors in the hope that the others involved will also do their part to care for the trails.

In the final analysis, this entails risk for the party who makes the initial effort. It is never possible to predict whether the concession one makes will also be reciprocated by the other party. When illegal contributions to a political party become public knowledge, and the general secretary of the party puts his own head on the block for the party chairman and resigns, he has the right to expect that he will later be rewarded with an appointment to the position of secretary of defense or secretary of labor—and yet he can't depend on it. This type of "advance payment," where there is no certainty that compensation for an up-front effort will actually be forthcoming, hinges on an attitude that plays an important role in informality: trust (see Luhmann, 1968: 48ff.).

The perpetuation and expansion of such trusting relationships can lead to the formation of loyalty networks, cliques, and old boy networks which result in members of the organization making long-term commitments to one another. When such networks are dominated by a single individual, organizational sociologist Horst Bosetzky, referring to the movie *The Godfather*, sees a Don-Corleone principle operating in administrations, businesses, hospitals, and political parties. Much like a Mafia don who creates loyalty among his subordinates by doing them favors, superiors accommodate employees by doing them favors so that they can rely on their loyalty at a later time (see Bosetzky, 1974).

When Bullying Suddenly Arises: Forms of Negative Sanctioning

When the exchange processes that normally transpire in an organization cease to function, negative attributions are quick to arise. The more innocuous formulations claim that the "chemistry" with the colleague isn't right, that so-and-so "plays it by the book" too much and makes a note in the file every time something is discussed. Someone else might be labeled an eager beaver, an overachiever, a sponger, or a telltale, and there are complaints that "you just can't work with a person like that."

Since informal expectations cannot be imposed formally, for example, by making reference to an official reprimand or dismissal, other means come into play. The colleague who "has an attitude" does not receive important information he in fact urgently needs to do his job. If a manager refuses to "cooperate," one stops covering her mistakes in front of other departments and simply lets her walk into a trap. If subordinates push for their formal rights too insistently, their superiors can resort to bossing—bullying from above—and withhold important resources which their subordinates need to perform their duties.

When imposing informal expectations, we must not overlook that it is also possible to draw on the resources available through an organization's formal structure. For example, due to their weak position in the hierarchy, the directors of vocational schools have difficulty imposing their expectations on teachers. Generally speaking, they do not have the power to dismiss a teacher, and their ability to affect the person's career is also very limited. Yet they do have one tool at their disposal to make cantankerous teachers conform, namely, assigning them to teach unpopular courses—subjects such as English or history for students taking "Introduction to Butchery" or "Intermediate Retail Meat Sales." If they still don't get the message, the teachers find themselves permanently shuttling from one class to the next until they either bring their behavior into line with the director's expectations or request a transfer to a different school.

Such sanctioning practices are often referred to as bullying. In the media they are also known as "psychological terror in the workplace," "workplace harassment," or "inhumane conduct among coworkers." Even though the individuals involved may interpret this behavior in terms of personal characteristics—the boss's sadism, the brutality of my colleagues, or the cruelty of my subordinates—from the perspective of organizational research it is interesting that bullying generally occurs in connection with an effort to establish informal norms within an organization. For the very reason that informal expectations can only be imposed through informal channels, sanctioning practices arise that the organization itself is almost incapable of preventing through directives, regulations, or handouts.

What to Do? Beyond the Dream of Shaping Organizational Culture

Among practitioners as well as in the research community, the concept of informality in the meantime has come to be viewed as old-fashioned. As a result, it is often silently replaced by the notion of organizational culture. The literature on organizational research— due perhaps to a lack of definitional ability, but perhaps also because of insufficient interest in precision—did not clarify what "culture" actually is, what it consists of, its characteristics, its effect, and how it should be studied. Consequently, it was possible to apply the terms informality and organizational culture interchangeably to one and the same phenomenon, namely, an organization's undecided decision premises.

A key reason that the concept of organizational culture was devised is because it could be used to reactivate a management dream that had already influenced many managers' thinking on the topic of informality. They dreamed of harnessing the informal networks, the concealed incentive structures, and implicit modes of thought for their own interests. Even the human relations approach had hopes of translating the many informal processes into formally accepted procedures. This would have done justice to human needs in the workplace while simultaneously discovering the key to increased efficiency (see Roethlisberger and Dickson, 1939). Ultimately, it was here that the idea of "technocratic formalism" evolved (Heydebrand, 1989: 343f.), which is aimed at giving management the ability to shape and control the many negotiations, implicit understandings and ad hoc agreements.

In particular, the best-selling book *In Search of Excellence* by organizational consultants Thomas J. Peters and Robert H. Waterman (1982) reactivated the idea of "soft factors" as shapeable success factors subsumed under the concept of organizational culture. It was a simple promise that fed management's hopes of exerting a formative influence. The success of an organization, the assumption ran, does not depend primarily on its formal structure, but rather on its culture. In the final analysis, it is identity, special knowledge, work style, and the permanent staff that determine an organization's rise or fall.

In order to transform the concept of informality into organizational culture, only two minor accents were shifted. First, the concept of organizational culture focused more strongly on typical cognitive styles, value systems, and patterns of perception, that is, on the undecidable decision premises of the organization. Deviations from the official rules and standards were comparatively neglected. After all, violating organizational guidelines, disregarding management directives, or the pursuit of goals which the organization had not agreed upon were tough recommendations to sell to organizational management. Second, the concept of culture, which originated in anthropology, was geared more toward emphasizing the special characteristics of individual "companies of excellence" as opposed to the many firms that fell short of that standard. The concept of culture underscores differences from other cultures, whereas that of informality primarily focuses on the differences from formality.

These two shifts in emphasis allowed organizational culture to serve as a magic bullet for a time. It was a management panacea that would supposedly enable one to address the growing control problems in companies, public administrations, schools, or hospitals. If the creation of decentralized units caused the centrifugal forces in an organization to increase, then organizational culture was supposed to hold the parts together. If the elimination of hierarchies made controlling employees more difficult, then it was organizational culture that had to constrain them. The concept became a kind of fetish that was used on the one hand to superficially renounce classical notions of control, while on the other hand allowing the preservation of a hidden belief in an order which, although somewhat difficult to access, was nevertheless controllable (see also the critique formulated by Luhmann, 2000: 239).

Yet one encounters the problem that management may indeed work on an ideal image of its organizational culture, lavish money on developing mission statements for its employees, and indulge itself in workshops offering orgies of humanistic prose, but there is no certainty that these cultural programs will also become permanent. Well-established thought patterns, value systems, and informal behavioral norms cannot be rationally controlled, formally programmed, and technocratically administered. Such is the character of undecided decision premises. An organizational culture emerges as an order as if of its own accord. That doesn't preclude change, but one cannot introduce a transformation of culture by decree (Luhmann, 2000: 243 and 245).

Even worse, when management espouses certain guiding principles and cultural values in festive speeches or high-gloss brochures, it always raises doubt in the target audience as to whether it might simply be a case of paying lip service. Organizational cultures are a little bit like sex: an excessive amount of talking about it gives rise to the suspicion that the person who is so keen on the discussion may be suffering from an acute lack of it. This explains why the base often reacts with cynicism to organizational culture programs designed from above. Instructions from senior management that workers must always carry a plastic card in their overalls with the company's latest mission statement, will garner subtle sarcasm on the assembly line.

But what are the options for changing organizational culture? What opportunities does management have to intervene? It sounds paradoxical, but the central mechanism for changing informality—or organizational culture, if you will—is to make decisions that affect the formal structure. It is not the case, as some control-enthusiasts in management might wish, that by announcing the formal structure one can simultaneously enact changes in the organizational culture. Rather, the change results from the fact that every shift in official reporting channels, every announcement of a new official target, every hire, transfer, or termination has an effect on the way work in the divisions, departments, or teams is informally coordinated.

Naturally, one can never predict exactly which effects a change in the formal structures will produce at the level of organizational culture, but research in organizational science has at least shown us how formal and informal expectations mesh and has indicated the direction in which certain characteristics of the formal structure will unfold their effects. A number of central questions lend themselves to this purpose.

How Strong is the Formalization of Expectations?

One of the main opportunities for intervention lies in determining how strongly the expectations are formalized in the first place. After all, organizations enjoy substantial latitude concerning the degree to which the expectations they place on their members are officially codified through programs, process manuals, lists of objectives, hierarchies, voting rules, and job descriptions.

One of the strategies might be to formalize as *many* expectations as possible, in other words, to make fulfilling them a controllable and enforceable condition of membership. To this end, detailed instructions are issued, and everyone is required to follow them. The entire organization is planned in the form of detailed targets— management by objectives—and compliance is strictly monitored.

A large amount of energy is expended on standardizing communications procedures and defining the circumstances that permit deviations from standardized communications.

The reasons for intensifying the formalization of expectations in this manner can vary widely. They range from senior executives having the impression that they are losing control, the desire for rationalization measures to trim the fat or take up the slack in the organization, or the hope that a very deep hierarchy will make it possible to hold individual persons accountable at all times. Sometimes there are legal reasons for reinforcing formalizations, for example, requirements that certain work processes be precisely documented. Nor is it uncommon that demands for formalization are expressed "from below." Ultimately, demands brought forward by employees for more orientation or greater security are often nothing but demands that the terms of membership be formulated more precisely.

Since the contradictory demands placed on organizations cannot be wedged into a consistent formal edifice of rules, the unavoidable effect of intensified formalization is an increase in violations. As an example, automobile manufacturers not only have very precise quality standards for the dashboards, steering wheels, or axles that are to be supplied; their certification requirements also have a substantial impact on their suppliers' production processes. Such intrusions by car manufacturers have become so rigid in the meantime, that suppliers are left with no alternative: parallel to the ever-growing standardization and formalization, they must increasingly routinize such deviations from the specifications as are required by production adjustments on short notice, and establish a second, unofficial system of controls.

The state-run enterprises in the former Eastern Bloc countries were a model case for illustrating the effects of overbearing formalization. Yet the special feature in the Eastern Bloc wasn't so much the bureaucratization of agreements within the companies themselves— in that respect the enterprises in command economies differed surprisingly little from those in market economies—but rather the bureaucratization of relations *between* the companies. A government planning agency predetermined the number and quality of the products a company had to produce, just as it determined which supplier parts the company would receive. As economist Joseph S. Berliner had already observed in the 1950s, this had the effect of creating an exchange-based "underlife" in the socialist planned economies. According to Berliner, the director of a company in the Soviet Union, the GDR, or Yugoslavia could only succeed if he engaged in any number of practices that were based on agreements between companies but were officially forbidden (see Berliner, 1957: 324).

Working with such decidedly over-regulated systems and their concurrent explosive rise in violations can be functional, for example, when the object is always to have a means of exerting pressure. To illustrate, government methadone programs generally subject the release of this heroin substitute to very strict controls. Each individual step of the treatment must be documented in detail. The methadone can only be dispensed in medical practices, and receipt of the medication occurs only under condition that the addict undergoes concurrent psychological counseling. These rigid legal requirements are often difficult to reconcile with the medical approach in the treatment of heavy drug users. The effect of the stringent regulations is that doctors disobey the rules, commit administrative violations, and break the law to ensure the program's success even in patients who are difficult to treat. While this constitutes an unpleasant situation for the individual physician, it provides the government a means to clamp down, which it almost never has because in other instances the medical profession is self-regulating.

Under Which Circumstances Does One Refrain from Formalization?

Proceeding in the opposite direction is also conceivable, however. Here, businesses, political parties, or initiatives refrain to a large degree from formalizing their expectations of members. Processes are not standardized, but adjusted by acclamation instead. Although targets are defined through common effort, they can be missed, modified, or even abandoned without violating the rules of membership. Authorized communication channels in terms of hierarchies, co-signing authority, or official group publications are defined only in broad strokes.

Instead, an effort is made to ensure that everyone can communicate with everyone else. In extreme cases, even the crossing of a formal threshold to membership becomes unnecessary to determine who is a member and who is not. Rather, influence (and also rewards in the form of money, opportunities for advancement, or social recognition) depends on the services one renders for the organization.

There are various reasons for largely abstaining from formalizations: frustration with bureaucratic over-management; the difficulty of motivating poorly paid or even unpaid employees in a strict, excessively regulated hierarchy; political convictions about the democratization of organizations; or the adoption of the latest ideas in reorganization that management gurus have concocted. Thus, efforts to deformalize organizations are not only encountered in leftist political groups or self-governing companies, but also among the founders of start-ups or the executives of major corporations who are receptive to the latest trends in management fashion.

Interestingly, however, forgoing formalization on a broad scale does not result in a situation where "anything goes." Instead, all organizational research indicates that tried and true practices establish themselves, patterns of cooperation emerge, and interpersonal networks form which in part work very well under pressure.

Since formalized criteria for joining or leaving such organizations barely exist, specific mechanisms for regulating membership develop. Becoming a member of these organizations often takes place through induction by close acquaintances in the individual's own network. Particularly in organizations which have dispensed with formalization to a large degree, there tend to be no fixed boundaries between personal relationships and those within the organization. A person's departure from the organization is often not brought about through coercion based on a violation of the membership rules, but is achieved by displaying hostility toward them.

Sociologist Jo Freeman (1972: 157f.) observed that when organizations waive formalized hierarchies, particularly at the top levels, outside sources impose a "star system" on them. The mass media need spokespeople who can provide information in the name of a political organization. Political parties need contacts among their potential coalition partners, people who can also implement agreements internally. Customers need a desk they can turn to if they have problems. If an organization itself forgoes creating such key positions, they will be defined from without. The mass media will target one particularly articulate individual within a grassroots political organization, even if the person has not been officially appointed as the spokesperson. If a political party has no leader, its coalition partners will negotiate with the person who comes closest to fulfilling their needs. If a company refrains from identifying a customer-care representative, the public will approach the person who happens to be available at the moment or has the highest visibility. The problem of such "star systems" is that the organization itself has no way of removing stars who have been designated by outside sources, except by creating leadership positions within a formalized hierarchy.

It is true that even loosely formalized organizations can easily be geared to achieving goals. People join together to ensure that everyone receives a basic income, they found a self-governing taxi business, or they start a dot-com with a dynamic image so they can attract as much venture capital as possible. Yet according to Freeman, the problem is that the lack of formalization produces organizations that are long on motivation but short on results. Freeman's research on feminist organizations showed that those with a low degree of formalization are good at "getting their members to talk," but bad at "getting things done."

What Becomes Formalized and How Does it Shape Informality?

Informal expectations, partially crystallized into organizational cultures, always emerge when problems arise that cannot be solved through directives (see Luhmann, 2000: 241) or, one might add, it is only through directives that informal expectations are created. In the final analysis, the purpose they serve is to balance out the rigidities that formal structures produce.

When *programs* are involved, for example, one can observe that rigid, formal if-then programming is often balanced out through an accumulation of informal goal programs and vice versa. As an illustration, classical conveyor belt production was conditionally programmed, but when the system was overloaded the assumption was that workers on the production line would not adhere strictly to the conditional programs, but also consider the urgency of filling the order and doing so precisely on time. We can assume that Taylorist organizations were only able to prevail because they were systematically undermined in operational practice. If blue and white collar workers had oriented themselves in their day-to-day activities to the official Taylorist system, the result would have been chaos according to a broad consensus in organizational science. This informal accommodation served as a source of influence for the workers in the organization and might explain why in many cases they vehemently resisted the introduction of partially autonomous workgroups, where they were required to produce at the same level, but now within the framework of a formal structure.

In the case of *communication channels*, one observes that organizations with numerous hierarchical levels seek balance through informality, and the multitude of levels is pared down to practicable dimensions. To speed up the process of reaching an understanding, immediate superiors are bypassed and methods of operation are agreed upon directly with superiors at the next higher level. In contrast, when very few hierarchical levels exist, distinct informal leadership cadres develop which also enable individuals at the same hierarchical level to negotiate agreement relatively quickly.

Such balancing mechanisms can also be observed in terms of *personnel*, for example, when an organizational role threatens to clash too severely with an outside role. For this reason, it is generally mandatory for attorneys, police officers, physicians, or therapists to refuse cases in which they have a personal stake—even though they will often informally monitor the matter. But the opposite can also be seen. When professional guidelines require such professionals to accept cases where they are personally involved, they try to make informal arrangements with colleagues and persuade them to become overall case managers. There are any number of TV series where the storyline is based largely on the tension inherent in this situation.

Consequently, one must always anticipate that the introduction of formal expectations will lead to the emergence of an informal counter structure to balance out the rigidities and supervision gaps entailed by formal expectations. Under such circumstances, informal expectations my well come to dominate daily life. But when conflict arises, one can always play a trump card by referring to the formal structure.

How Does One Switch Between Formality and Informality?

In practice, switching back and forth between formality and informality goes on all the time. When an oral request for information is received from another department, one either declines the request or asks that it be routed through official channels, or one can be collegial and provide an informal answer to the question. One either discusses a process with one's superior in formal terms, thereby risking an official refusal, or one keeps the tone of the conversation on the informal side, so that the request can be introduced again at a more favorable time (see Luhmann, 1964: 117).

The interplay between formal and informal structures can be viewed as a key characteristic of organizations as compared to other social institutions such as marriages, groups, nations, or social movements. The relationship between formal and informal components gives rise to a very curious style of cooperation. Arguments are conducted with great discipline and sensitivity, because even when conflicts are carried out one must always bear in mind that cooperation in a formal sense will be ongoing (Luhmann, 1964: 246).

As Niklas Luhmann observed early on (Luhmann, 1964: 246f.), opportunities for informal modes of cooperation lend organizations a certain lightness. Arguments needn't be settled immediately through formal decisions; there are opportunities to gauge one's strength informally. Ongoing business operations often produce new solutions and new power relationships which can be sustained over the longer term without formal safeguards. Formal decisions—the promotion of an executive who has unofficially outgrown her rank in the hierarchy—then simply serve as ratification of conditions that are already present.

At the same time, the existence of a formal order prevents the organization from becoming balkanized and collapsing amidst informal conflicts that seem unwilling to end (see Luhmann, 1964: 247). All of the participants realize that conflicts can ultimately be settled through a formal decision. As a result, parties involved in open conflict often tone down the intensity of the controversy, realizing that matters can be settled at the next higher level of the hierarchy if necessary. Still, since they are uncertain of the outcome of a formal decision, and because they are aware that members of a hierarchy are reluctant to settle conflicts in that manner, it is relatively rare for them to utilize the option of formalizing a settlement. In spite of that, it is an option that continues to shape the way the members of an organization coexist with one another.

THE DISPLAY ASPECT: ORGANIZATIONAL HYPOCRISY

As an outsider, the first description of a corporation, a government agency, a university, or hospital to reach one's eyes or ears often seems extraordinarily smooth. When one visits a company, the firm's qualities are extolled; at career fairs, agencies and hospitals have nothing but the highest praise for themselves as employers. In their fund-raising efforts, aid organizations such as UNICEF, Amnesty International, or Oxfam make a point of underscoring their internal administrative efficiency and generate good publicity by obtaining certification through outside review agencies.

There are any number of journalists who fall for these slick corporate presentations. It is a standard complaint among journalists that the members of organizations immediately switch to whitewashing as soon as they are asked questions about conditions on the inside. Faced with a more or less organized cartel of silence toward the press, journalists rework materials prepared by the organizations into articles of their own, rather than having nothing at all to put down on paper. This often results in tiresome reporting on officially announced sales figures, turnover, or profits, as well as in commentaries that are informed by a fairly naïve understanding of organizations and regularly call for greater ethics or greater sensitivity to customers. Or, it produces service journalism that is reminiscent of the yellow press, where reporting focuses on which hotels today's managers are using, which golf courses they prefer, and the kind of body lotion they use.

There are also a number of academics who believe that the answers supplied by the management of organizations in response to questionnaires that researchers have sent to them, actually reflect organizational realities—as opposed to the reality the respondents believe that the researchers would like to see. Consequently, it is not uncommon for academic research to create the impression in readers that organizations are closely attuned to the pulse of the times and are diligently striving to implement the values that are currently in vogue. In the final analysis, many a scholarly article that outlines what is needed for success in world-class corporations—based on the survey responses of top decision makers—probably causes amusement among those who know those very world-class corporations from the inside.

What lies behind these polished portrayals of organizations? How can we approach them analytically? What functions do they fulfill in the organizations?

Sprucing up the Organization

Sprucing up describes a process through which organizations attempt to present a coherent and convincing picture of themselves by issuing vetted reports, intricate organizational charts, clearly represented process flows, or polished statements. Complexity and unresolved conflicts are screened out, and in their deceptive slipstream a second reality, bearing only a very limited relationship to the actual processes within the respective organizations, is created for the external world. The onlooker is confronted with a harmonious total work of art while on the inside the members are improvising, arguing, and not infrequently blundering (see Neuberger, 1994).

We know this process of enhancing presentations from other situations as well. One can observe that two people who are supposedly deep in conversation will try to "present" themselves the moment they notice that someone is watching them. The street demonstrations held by the peace, environmental, and feminist movements are often carefully crafted stage productions of political concerns. Groups of adolescents who loiter at supermarkets to panhandle a dollar or two from passers-by may not be presenting themselves exactly in the way their parents might find ideal, but based on the remove they show from middle-class norms, they are often exceptionally gifted at projecting an image. Families who move in the public eye sometimes present such a perfect picture of familial happiness that their friends are surprised when they suddenly break up.

Such façades of social structures do not simply exist; first they have to be constructed and expanded, maintained and improved if required (see Luhmann, 1964: 113). In groups, families, or even protest movements, the façades often appear to be the result of improvisation, sudden inspiration, or expectation patterns that have been adopted without examination. They emerge in a spontaneous manner in organizations as well, for example, when two coworkers suddenly and intuitively change the subject the moment a client joins them, or when a new member of the organization tries to guess how the dress code changes when an important guest is present. Yet in organizations, cultivation of the façade is also frequently addressed in a coordinated and deliberate manner. Regulations are issued to define the way one should behave toward customers, clients, or cooperating partners. Cadres of façade specialists are created in the form of press, communications, and marketing departments, and they, in turn, employ outside service providers such as advertising agencies, PR firms, and interior designers. In organizational research, the systematic, planned construction and development of façades is aptly referred to as "impression management."

The Presentational Function of Façades

A façade is an organization's way of expressing how it wants to be perceived. Through the conscious or unconscious copying processes of their members, organizations form their own linguistic conventions which provide security in dealing with the outside world. Letterheads, official seals, and websites concomitantly serve as symbols which the organization uses not only to achieve ongoing recognition, but always as an attempt to express something as well. Just as a family's living room often also serves as its "showroom," organizations have facilities that are furnished in keeping with the image they display toward non-members. An organization's dress code can support the external image created by these spaces, but it also offers the advantage of not being tied to the rooms themselves so that one can make a real impression on suppliers, customers, or partners with relatively little overhead. This aspect of façades may be referred to as their decorative or presentational function.

In their façades, organizations frequently draw on cross-organizational examples of architectural design, dress codes, and language usage. It is striking how many corporations, government agencies, hospitals, and universities have turned caretakers, secretaries, and cleaning ladies into facility managers, administrative assistants, and custodians. It is surprising how quickly the styles of dress considered acceptable in terms of an external presentation can gain traction beyond the boundaries of an organization. For instance, pantsuits for women have now become acceptable in the mosaic of organizational façades, at least in Western countries, and no longer evoke enraged protest. Organizations frequently also strive to develop their own specific set of symbols in an effort to delineate themselves from other organizations. The written language of bureaucracy, a form of expression that is used by government agencies and seems stilted at first, needn't necessarily be interpreted as the result of "ineradicable habitual usage by subordinate bureaucrats," but carries "symbolic value for the ideal presentation" of the work that public administrations produce. By virtue of that, it serves as a means of delineating them from other organizations (see Luhmann, 1964: 113f.).

As a rule, organizations try to present as consistent a picture of themselves as possible. Buzzwords such as "corporate design," "corporate communications," or "corporate publishing" conceal an attempt to standardize an organization's set of symbols sufficiently to ensure that outsiders recognize the organization frequently and quickly. Ideally, corporate design as applied to a range of things such as coffee mugs, ballpoint pens, and landscaping is meant to convey a unified image of the enterprise. On the other hand, an organization can also pursue the strategy of contrasting its diversity with the consistency of its outward appearance. In that case, instead of stressing the uniformity of gray suits for both men and women, the differing styles of dress and speech within the organization are used to signal that it encompasses various types of people, and that this accounts for its uniqueness.

The Protective Function of Façades

Façades also perform a second important task, namely, shielding the internal sectors of an organization. The idea is to obstruct the view of outsiders so that one can prepare decisions carefully, hide potential conflicts from the outside world, or conceal mistakes and embarrassments. This could be called the cover-up function of façades.

Generally speaking, organizations do not disclose to outsiders the exact details of a manufacturing process, the makings of an administrative decision, or the planning of seminar offerings at a university. The object is not only to conceal the minor deviations from the rules that occur in the form of tricks, schemes, and shortcuts. Even many processes that are entirely above board are only suitable for outsiders to a limited degree (see Luhmann, 1964: 114). The legitimacy of political decisions would be further eroded if voters received detailed information on how often decisions are the result of wheeling and dealing between the parties.

It is particularly important that, wherever possible, mistakes do not become "part of the record." Under no circumstances must they become public knowledge because, according to Niklas Luhmann (1964: 114), "manifest errors are much more flawed than secret ones." This is one of the key reasons why descriptions of organizations portray their ventures as successes for as long as possible. One concedes that everything didn't go as planned and that unexpected obstacles were encountered, but ultimately the undertaking is presented as a success.

Organizations can attempt to structure their internal processes in such a way that they bear up under external scrutiny. Producers of high-end automobiles construct "transparent factories" where interested buyers can follow every step of the assembly. Political parties allow internal conflicts to leak out in order to demonstrate that members with different positions can reconcile their views with one another. Organizations attempt to build trust by suggesting to observers that they are getting a look behind the scenes. But despite efforts to create transparency, the fact remains unchanged that certain details of the inner processes must be kept hidden from the view of non-members. To achieve that end, a second backdrop is created behind the scenes which the spectators are allowed to see.

Hiding the Façade as a Façade

There are situations when all of the participants clearly realize that an organization is decking itself out. When the government runs full-page advertisements in daily newspapers praising its own labor market, health, or defense policies, readers understand that the intention is to convince them of its policies—with the support of the taxpayers' money. Yet in most situations it is useful for an organization if its façade is not immediately recognizable for what it is.

On the one hand, this is because the decorative function of façades is often particularly effective when the beholder does not recognize the façade as such to begin with. One need only consider the barbed remarks journalists make when they realize that the comments coming from their dialogue partner are all too transparently based on a façade. They might point out, for example, that the president of a baseball club is reading "his opinion" from a sheet of paper—apparently because there were difficulties agreeing on an official statement within the club. Or they might make the smug observation that the chairman of a political party "appears to be relaxed"—thereby suggesting that his agitation is still clearly visible.

On the other hand, according to Niklas Luhmann, the cover-up function requires that façades must hide the fact that they are hiding something (see Luhmann, 1964: 115). To illustrate, assume that a nearly 100-page internal field manual of a consultant firm regulates not only the color of employees' socks, the quality of their suits, and the height of their heels, but also expressly demands that in cases of assignments involving longer periods of time spent at a client's firm, consultants must never, as a matter of principle, leave the office before the client even if they have nothing more to do. It makes sense that the existence of the handbook should not come to the client's awareness. It is inconsistent with an outward display for the observer to recognize screening, concealment, and cover-ups all too quickly.

But why do organizations create façades in the first place? Why doesn't every day qualify as open house day for companies, government agencies, or political parties?

The Benefits of Hypocrisy

Since façades represent the aspect of the organization that is presented to the outside world, their functionality must be sought in the expectations that are being placed on the organization from without.

Cushioning the Impact of Contradictory Demands

An initial motive for the construction of a façade lies in the contradictory demands that organizations are required to meet simultaneously. A conservative political party must reach out to its traditional voter base in rural areas, while at the same time retaining its appeal for high-tech oriented urban voters. It must at least create the impression that it deserves to be called "conservative," while at the same time allowing its voters to adopt a contemporary lifestyle.

Naturally, if an organization found itself in this kind of double-bind, it could simply choose one side over the other. Many a manager dreams that the contradictory demands placed on his organization would dissolve, and it would be possible—with the active support of organizational consultants—to focus every company, church, or university on one specific goal such as selling mobile phones as profitably as possible, gaining salvation for the faithful, or achieving 100 percent "customer satisfaction" among the students of a university. This would indeed fulfill demands for purity and consistency, yet at the same time one would lose support in many areas of society. The logic behind the decision is simple: if one reaches a fundamental decision that favors the one side, then the other will remain dissatisfied, and that poses a high risk for the organization.

As a result, organizations fine-tune their façades so they can at least superficially fulfill the varying demands placed upon them. For every relevant topic, they craft a specific position that is as attractive as possible for their surroundings, include it in their external presentation, but fail to mention the potential conflicts between positions on the respective subjects. To that end, organizations create the role of a speaker for each segment of their environment. In turn, each respective role develops its own linguistic conventions for governmental contacts, the mass media, or the capital markets, as examples. Or, organizations will determine which interest group in their environment requires particular attention in the current situation, and make a point of meeting its demands—later switching their emphasis to other interest groups.

The more contradictory the expectations that an organization faces, the higher the demands are on the façade. Thus, the more a corporation is confronted with the demands of major shareholders, the government, labor unions, environmental initiatives, and, not least, its own customers, the greater the value it will place on presenting itself as a company that is simultaneously profitable in the short term, employee oriented, environmentally conscious, socially committed, and which conducts a sustainable business to boot.

Façades Reduce Internal Conflict

A second motive for constructing façades lies in the necessity of protecting internal conflicts. Internal debate over the best way to do things, internal criticism of strategies developed by top-level management, and knowledge of the unintended side effects produced by executive decisions are things that exist in every organization. Generally speaking, these conflicts do not have to do with members being driven by personal motives or competitive impulses. Rather, the reason is simply because they come into contact with different segments of the environment and hold different positions in the organization, and therefore develop different, often conflicting perspectives.

Of course, an organization could also put out the message that "we have no secrets." A global company which has just formed from the merger of two automobile manufacturers and is experiencing vehement internal debate over whether the merger made sense, could abstain from concealing the conflict from the public. Nevertheless, when conflicts become known they result in a loss of legitimacy for the organization in its environment. When news of internal strife gets out, some of the more innocuous comments might include, "They can't agree with each other," "They're at war with each other," or "They don't know what they're doing."

Furthermore, when observations of that kind come from the outside, they aggravate the conflicts within. The environment works like an amplifier. With every comment from the outside world, conduct inside the organization becomes less civil, and as a result the organization increasingly loses the possibility of regulating the conflict on its own. When internal conflicts escalate, it is sometimes reminiscent of celebrity marriages that run into trouble: the mass media eagerly feed on every quarrel, thereby only making the crisis worse.

This explains why organizations construct a façade and make sure that their conflicts, doubts, and uncertainties remain hidden from view. Over the course of years, the merger of the two automobile companies is portrayed to the outside world as a major coup, even while the internal blame game is in progress and people are being held responsible for the disaster. To illustrate, after the merger of Daimler and Chrysler the company overall was at times worth less than Daimler alone had been beforehand. The shareholders' dissatisfaction over the destruction of capital was adeptly countered by referring to the irrationality of the capital markets and thereby diverting attention from the internal strife.

Dissimulation and Hypocrisy

It becomes obvious that organizations must always remain aware of two things. On the one side, they are under constraint to find as rational a structure as possible for their internal processes—making evaluable administrative decisions, producing fast cars, or generating innovative research results. On the other side, they feel under obligation, as it were, to always satisfy the demands for political, legal, economic, and scientific legitimacy raised by their environment. To quote organizational sociologists John Meyer and Brian Rowan (1977), we can speak of the necessity for both a "technical" as well as an "institutional rationality."

The problem is that demands for a streamlined production of administrative decisions, automobiles, or research findings are frequently incompatible with demands stemming from the organization's institutional environment. Structuring the internal workings of an organization efficiently often conflicts with outside demands for environmentally friendly production methods, shareholders' cries for rationalization, or the desire to have the production structure align with the most current management styles.

For these reasons, all organizations—ruling parties as well as the political opposition, multinational economic development organizations as well as the NGOs that are critical of globalization, major automobile manufacturers as well as their labor unions or employee representatives—always rely on a polished self-presentation to their environment, in addition to their actual services. We can call it "necessary window dressing," "unavoidable self-embellishment," or "the knack of self-portrayal." However, one can also join organizational scientist Nils Brunsson (1989) in speaking more directly about the necessity for "dissimulation" and "hypocrisy" present in every organization.

Commonalities and Differences between the Display Aspect and the Formal Aspect

At first glance, an organization's external display aspect, its idealized self-portrayal, bears similarities to its formal structure, in other words, the order of the organization. Often described using the metaphor of a machine, the formal structure focuses on assigning clear responsibilities and creating processes that are as predictable as possible. Public administrations attach great value to showing that they are doing nothing more than implementing political decisions, that the determinations they make comply with official procedure, and that all citizens are treated according to the same criteria.

Although it is certainly correct that an organization's formal structure is often well suited for presentation to the outside world, it would be wrong to represent the formal structure as *the* display aspect of the organization. In corporations, government agencies, hospitals, or NGOs, the display aspect and the formal aspect often diverge. The explanation for this lies in the different demands placed on the two sides of an organization.

The Reasons for Separating the Display Aspect from the Formal Aspect

As we have shown, organizations use their façades to make a favorable impression on a wide range of constituents—customers, suppliers, cooperating partners, competitors, politicians, journalists, job seekers—all are meant to receive as favorable an impression as possible. Yet ideas on what constitutes such an impression diverge significantly among target audiences. Thus, an organization can't be too specific in what it displays. While every concrete statement is sure to impress one group of people, it will frighten others away.

For this reason, it is detrimental if an organization sets too high a standard for *consistency* in its external presentation. All of the demands for legitimation that are being made by the environment simply cannot be filled at the same time. Organizations are often criticized for escaping into abstractions and nebulous imagery, but from this perspective their flight does not result from bad intentions, insufficient intellectual ability, or even a lack of professionalism. Instead, it is caused by the very demands that are imposed from the outside.

The demands placed on the organization's formal aspect are opposite in nature. The formal structure serves as a way of articulating the expectations placed on members, and this necessitates *concretization*. It is only when a sales employee is required to sell a concrete number of products, as opposed to merely achieving customer satisfaction, that her work can be managed, coordinated, and monitored.

At the same time, this assumes that the formalized expectations of members are highly *consistent*. Contradictions in formal programs or communication channels are only permissible to a limited degree, because the activities of the organization's members cannot be regulated through contradictory expectations. Otherwise members would always invoke the rule that happened to accommodate them, and there would be no way to hold them responsible for infractions against the prevailing order (see Luhmann, 1964: 155).

This explains why individual elements of the formal structure can indeed be used to construct and expand an organization's façade. Yet the mere presentation of the goals that structure the members' activities, the formally dictated hierarchy, and the official criteria for recruitment into or termination from the organization are enough to create an effective façade. As contact with the environment occurs, these elements of the formal structure must be supplemented by general value statements, enhanced portrayals of communication channels, and an embellished rendering of the reality of membership.

Programs, Communication Channels, Personnel: Where the Display Aspect and the Formal Aspect Diverge

It is true that *programs* can be suitable for use in presentations to · the outside world. When a bank announces that it has set a goal of returning 15 percent on investment in the coming year, it creates legitimacy with its investors. As a rule, however, an organization's goals, let alone the resources expended to achieve them, are not fully disclosed to non-members. For example, the bank's incentive structure is kept confidential; it would enable outsiders to deduce the means that the organization intends to use to reach its goal of a fifteen percent return. After all, a client of the bank would lose confidence if he were to learn that his investment adviser had been instructed to sell the financial product that was just offered to him (and is particularly lucrative for the bank) even if it doesn't match his investment strategy. Thus, organizations always present to their environments only a limited, idealized, and overly harmonious selection of the goals they are supposedly striving to reach (see Luhmann, 1964: 112). Instead of prioritizing their goals unequivocally: "The most important thing is to bring unemployment down to five percent. We will spend money on our armed forces only when we've achieved that."

They present the external world with enumerations of values, thereby suggesting that all good things can be achieved at the same time. The portrayal of goals in an organization's external presentation implies, as political scientist Robert Packenham (1973: 123ff.) aptly observed, that "All good things go together."

At first glance, an organization's formal *communication channels* also seem to be well suited for external presentations. Many corporations, public administrations, and hospitals post their organizational charts—and consequently the communication channels their members are required to use—on their websites, where they can be downloaded. Most corporations, governmental agencies, and NGOs from the developing world realize that a PowerPoint slide (as slick as possible) of their organizational chart is important for their dealings with cooperating partners in industrialized countries because it creates the impression that decisions are made through established communication channels. But oftentimes organizations are not satisfied with having their external presentations reference their formal communication channels. For many organizations, part of making and managing impressions is to portray their hierarchies as flat—regardless of how the communication channels are actually structured. Even organizations that have as many as nine levels of hierarchy for five thousand employees—and often with good reason—like to praise themselves for their flat hierarchies. In their mission statements, public administrations proclaim their short communication pathways, even if senior officers reference the internal rules of procedure and remain warily attentive that the decision-making process does not simply bypass them.

Similarly, citing the qualities of an organization's *personnel* often creates a good impression in an external presentation. Influential certification industries have arisen to equip personnel with proof of legitimacy, thereby increasing the level of trust placed in the organization. Schools hire only "state-certified" teachers, nursing homes point to their "licensed attendants," and financial firms display their "certified financial auditors" (see Meyer and Rowan, 1977: 344). In addition to the official certifications, the particularly prestigious qualities of individual staff members are frequently emphasized. Some corporations present their newly recruited top managers in a style that reminds one of a soccer club presenting a newly acquired, up-and-coming Brazilian star—replete with press release, press conference, and exclusive interviews for key media. And yet there is much information about an organization's personnel that would be relevant to the organization itself but is not suited for an external presentation. Insights into the public personnel file are tightly controlled. If possible, difficult periods in a member's bio are concealed from the public; the illegitimate contacts that led to the hiring of an employee are kept under wraps. As a result, external presentations often tend to use somewhat flowery language that underscores the members' integrity and years of experience, without documenting precise facts or specific details.

The Solution: Decoupling

Since the display aspect and the formal aspect are each subject to different demands, organizations have no option but to decouple their "formalized internal core processes" from the "surface structures" that can be perceived externally. The organization's "talk" is only loosely connected with the "decision-making" level (see Brunsson, 1989: 32).

It is only such decoupling that gives organizations the freedom necessary to continue functioning in spite of the contradictory expectations they confront. Decoupling enables them to maintain the structures which appear legitimate and conform to their institutional environment, while in parallel focusing the day-to-day activities of their members on concrete demands.

Commonalities and Differences between the Display Aspect and Informality

Managers wish that organizations' informal processes and daily routines were suitable for external presentation as well. After all, it would make a CEO's job easier if she knew that she could allow visitors to roam through the organization and that they would later return to her deeply impressed by the motivation of the employees, their professional attitude, and their smooth cooperation with one another.

It is precisely this dream of a high degree of coherence between the display aspect and the informal aspect which is expressed in the almost naïve celebration of organizational culture by many managers, consultants, and researchers. The assumption is that the processes which develop beyond an organization's official work structure will naturally also be suitable for representing it to the outside world. Organizational culture, so the thinking goes, reflects the shared values, attitudes, and practices of the members, and these can be passed along in unfiltered form to the outside world.

Why Informal Processes are so Poorly Suited for External Presentations

Granted, there may be cases where informal processes are also suitable for external presentations. When the president visits the players' locker room after the team has won a world championship game, he would probably be taken aback to find a line of smartly dressed men. Rather, he will be expecting to encounter a horde of exuberant and boisterous players whose behavior will hardly be affected by his presence. Still, as a rule, informal processes rarely lend themselves to external presentations.

Particularly when the informal processes involve obvious deviations from an organization's formal rules and regulations, or even entail breaking the law, such practices do not make an especially good impression in an external presentation. As an example, there are good reasons why the informal practices that establish themselves in the maintenance crews responsible for changing the light bulbs at airports, repairing the escalators, or servicing the ticket machines in parking lots, are not officially made public. In spite of the firm's official policies on the reduction of inventory costs, the teams create "illegal stock rooms" that enable them to handle repair assignments on short notice. Over the course of the years, they appropriate ventilation rooms, storage space under escalators, and former vehicle maintenance areas in addition to the workshops they rent from the airport administration. This serves a purpose for the team and for the facilities management company as a whole. But such practices are poorly suited for an external presentation that is geared to the airport administration (as the company's primary client), to visitors from supply companies, or even to the company's own senior executives.

In corporations, public administrations, universities, or political parties, exposure to the public seems almost automatically to trigger an internal censorship mechanism. As soon as non-members are received in the form of customers, cooperating partners or competitors, the employees begin to extol the organization's supposedly hitch-free internal cooperation. In their remarks to the non-members, employees pay homage to the organizational values which are said to be shared by all, so that visitors who take a tour, or those attending presentations or workshops, sometimes have the impression that they are participating in near-religious events.

If an organization's informal processes are so poorly suited for external representation, which other functions might informality fulfill in the management of the display aspect?

Imposing the Display Aspect Through Informal Expectations

Even though informality may be poorly suited for the external image, it nevertheless plays an important role in bringing the members of the organization into line with its coherent presentation to the outside world. It is, of course, correct that an organization can define minimal standards for its members with respect to its external image. By offering no table service and using rather bright light and uncomfortable chairs in its stores, McDonald's may be pursuing the goal of getting rid of customers as quickly as possible, once they have made their purchase. Yet the company attempts to force its employees to display a pleasant attitude toward customers by requiring adherence to a catalog of conduct rules. Employees are instructed—with reference to the terms of employment—to behave in a friendly manner toward customers by using everything from an engaging greeting, to prefabricated responses to complaints, and a prescribed formula of thanks when the purchase is concluded.

According to Niklas Luhmann's observations however, such formalized presentation requirements get caught up in the relatively drastic cases and don't move beyond the "external aspects of behavior," in other words, clothing, jewelry, and greeting phrases. They do not reach the "more subtle sphere" where plausible presentations are produced (Luhmann, 1964: 121). It is indeed possible to forbid employees from arguing with one another when customers are present, but it is almost impossible to prevent employees from showing subtle signs of disliking each other, even in the presence of customers. It is likewise possible to enforce that members affirm the *goal* of the organization in external presentations, be it converting non-believers, schooling the uneducated, or selling cars to the non-motorized. Yet it is virtually impossible to make them project enthusiasm when they do so. In Luhmann's view, one can insist that "a person approach a superior with respect and due deference," but it is impossible to prevent "a subordinate from doing so in a manner that conveys to his superior, and anyone who might be watching, the real nature of his attitude" toward the organization's *hierarchy* (Luhmann, 1964: 121).

Consequently, in constructing and maintaining its façade an organization must also rely on informal pressure among colleagues. In terms of the external presentation, each member of the organization "is kept on track by his colleagues." "He will not find any co-players for deviations," because by engaging in open conflicts with colleagues, making disparaging remarks about the organization, or by "divulging damaging information," he will undermine the laboriously constructed self-presentation of his colleagues vis-à-vis outsiders (see Luhmann, 1964: 122).

According to Luhmann, "the more delicate and sensitive the presentation problems," the more the formal behavioral expectations that have been articulated as terms of membership and pertain to the external presentation must be supported through informal expectations among coworkers. "Formal directives" may still be able to make an airline present itself as modern or ensure that a hospital creates a hygienic impression. But this route does not lead to success with "the more delicate problems." For a "bank to appear trustworthy," for an "authority to appear to have a sense of justice," or a "brokerage to seem resourceful," it "requires a high degree of tactful collaboration on the overall image." While this can be "sketched out in advance" through formal expectations, "they alone will not be capable of actually creating it" (Luhmann, 1964: 122).

The Solution: The Presentation of Informality

Nonetheless, we must not overlook the fact that organizations gain legitimacy when their external presentations do not make artificial, contrived impressions. The (supposedly) spontaneous friendliness an employee expresses when interacting with a customer is generally more effective than the solicitude of call-center workers, which is immediately recognizable as part of their training. The magic word is "authenticity" which is supposed to make employees—and of late especially consultants as well—shine in their dealings with outside contacts.

This is the reason why organizations construct façades that pretend to permit a deep look inside their organizational culture, which is to say, the attitudes, informal practices, and shared value systems of their employees. Outsiders are promised "insight into the problematic areas as well" and "candid reporting, even on failures."

Yet it is precisely this kind of external presentation for which intensive internal preparations are made. There is keen debate as to which problem areas can be presented, and in what manner, and which of them—all candor notwithstanding—are best concealed from visitors. Steps are taken to ensure that the "authentic real-life descriptions" still convey a positive impression of the organization in spite of their authenticity and, further, that reports about failures conclude with a happy ending.

Naturally, it must not be noticeable that constructing the presentation of the organization's culture was arduous. After all, everyone is meant to believe that they are receiving somewhat haphazard insights into the real world of the organization. The paradox one encounters in managing an external image is that the very authenticity, spontaneity, and naturalism often require the most intensive preparation.

What to Do? Managing an Organization's Triple Reality

The greater the discrepancy between the members' official reality, that is, the reality they are *meant to practice*, and the reality they *actually practice*, the louder the voice of complaint will be heard. Corporations that embrace environmental protection in colorful brochures, while continuing to operate pollution-spewing facilities, will be accused of hypocrisy. Labor unions that push for job security and pay increases while at the same time pursuing austerity measures, often at the cost of their own employees, will be accused of dissembling. Criticism will be heard that there is often a distinct difference between the menu, the dish that comes to the table, and the taste of the food.

The direction of such criticism is clear: management should kindly practice what it preaches. According to the dominant view, mission statements, visions, value systems, and programs must be coupled as closely as possible with an organization's formal decisions—and also with its concrete practices. This mantra underlies all criticism of corporations and political parties and is ideally suited as a basic premise for media commentaries. First, if one observes that, "Their actions don't line up with their claims," one will always be right. Second, it is an easy way to earn brownie points with the audience, because there appears to be a meta-consensus—or a meta-hypocrisy—to the extent that there should be no disparity between word and deed (see Brunsson, 2003: 210ff.).

When top executives come under pressure in this manner, they sometimes allow themselves to get carried away and vocally come out in favor of authenticity. The tenor of their remarks is, "You have to say what you think, and do as you say." "This is real business, not just show business." But even the creed-like quality of the statement could make an observer suspicious. It is all too obvious here that a remark is being used instrumentally, as a trust-building measure, and can therefore simply be taken as yet another building block in the embellishment of an organizational façade.

What Are the Reactions to Cracks in the Façade? The Increased Affirmation of Values

Organizations conduct "presentation hygiene" on a regular basis. Every three years, they spend enormous amounts of money on certifying their efforts to provide equal opportunities for both men and women, the handicapped and non-handicapped, and foreign as opposed to native citizens, thereby ensuring that the organization achieves particularly high rankings on the media's diversity management lists (see Luhmann, 1996b: 64ff.).

Such presentation hygiene notwithstanding, an organization's façade can easily develop cracks. Legitimation crises of this kind require the organization to intensify its affirmation of relevant moral values. When the mass media report that children in Catholic institutions were subjected to routine physical abuse, then the bishop who stands publicly accused of bearing responsibility for the beatings must affirm that he is "fundamentally opposed to interpersonal violence" and that "he is deeply convinced, as an individual and as a Christian," that every human being should treat others in the same way he or she would like to be treated.

Often, as external criticism mounts, affirmations of value also seem to become more vocal. One could almost develop a search scheme. The more decisively an organization speaks out in public to avow its commitment to environmental protection, human rights, gender equality, or profitability, the greater its difficulties appear to be in living up to those same aspirations. It appears that the better the manners, the worse the matter they conceal.

Organizational researcher Nils Brunsson (2003) refers to this mechanism as "reverse coupling." According to Brunnson, "official reality" and "practiced reality" are not only decoupled, but actually exist in an inverse relationship to one another. As Brunnson sees it, problems encountered in living up to values such as environmental protection, human rights, or efficiency almost automatically lead to stronger affirmation of those very values. The higher the national debt, the louder the politicians will proclaim that it is unacceptable for us to pass along debts that our children will be unable to repay. But there is a problem with these affirmations of values: they're cheap (see Meyer, 1979: 494). Therefore, organizations must take different measures to reassure legitimacy.

How Can Legitimacy be Produced by Changing Formal Structures?

Organizations that find themselves in legitimation crises are often required to change their structures as a result. In doing so, they incur high costs which are then presented as evidence that they are serious about the undertaking. In economic science, such costly structural changes are referred to as "signaling"—sending out signals to generate legitimation (Spence, 1974). There are several approaches an organization can take.

Frequently, organizations will change their principal *programs* only if they are under enormous pressure to legitimize themselves. As an example, a radical transformation of goal programs tends to be the exception. Even in the wake of an environmental catastrophe that killed several thousand people, it is rather rare for a chemical company to mutate into an environmental protection group. As a general rule, the existing set of goal programs undergoes modifications. The chemical company decides to add the percentage of its revenues invested in environmental protection as a future evaluation criterion.

One commonly practiced method is to vary the resources an organization devotes to achieving its goals. It is a well-documented fact that organizations which find themselves under legitimation pressure are the ones most likely to try out new programs. The introduction of Japanese production methods such as the rationalization technique of lean management, the quality improvement method of *kaizen*, or the logistical concept of *kanban* are most likely to be detected in firms that have come under economic pressure and must therefore signal their shareholders that they are responding actively (Strang and Soule, 1998: 274).

The *communication channels* are another area where an organization can begin its attempt to increase legitimacy, because restructuring this aspect can also serve to express a shift in priorities. A frequent reaction to legitimacy crises is to elevate individual units to a higher level within the hierarchy, thereby signaling that from now on the problems will be handled by top management itself. Thus, one can observe that companies which have been rocked by major corruption scandals order their compliance departments to report to higher levels of the hierarchy than before; this signals to the outside world that they are willing to learn from the misconduct.

A further, knee-jerk reaction to a fundamental legitimacy crisis is a change in *personnel*. Particularly in mass-media portrayals, negative events—positive ones as well—are often linked to individuals because it allows for especially impressive reporting. But since organizations, as opposed to, say, royal families or rock bands, are able to replace their personnel, separating from certain individuals with as much public attention as possible poses an option for regaining legitimacy and steering the organization back into calmer waters. In this kind of reaction, political parties, corporations, and government institutions are essentially no different from a football team. In times of crisis, they replace the coach, not because they expect a different trainer will do a better job, but because replacing their leadership personnel is the only means they have to restore the confidence of their fan base, the players, and the media.

The tendency to change personnel when a crisis of legitimacy arises is understandable. The replacement of a top executive generates broad media coverage and is therefore a better method of maintaining an organization's external presentation than, for example, a political platform repeatedly extolling the family as the "nucleus of society," a bank releasing a new anticorruption mission statement on its website, or the formulation of cooperation guidelines between a company's board of directors and the staff association. Using the public removal of a senior executive as a pledge of improvement remains one of the most effective forms of organized hypocrisy.

Conclusion

Organizations will not be able to do without a loose coupling between "official reality," that is, the reality which the members are "required to practice," and reality as it is "actually practiced"—in other words between talk, decisions, and action. It is only such loose coupling that will provide the opportunity to stabilize their external presentation, with its striving for legitimation, while at the same time reacting to the current demands of day-to-day operations—or conversely, to refurbish their façade during legitimation crises without having to change their entire internal structure.

Nevertheless, the relationships between symbolic surface structure, formal structure, and operative deep-structure cannot be entirely decoupled. If a concern such as Siemens appoints an anticorruption officer, with much media fanfare, then the tried and true, economically well-justifiable, practice of bribery cannot continue in the same manner.

Thus, managing the triple reality of organizations entails not only engineering the decoupling of official reality from reality as it is actually practiced, in order to gain the advantages of flexibility for the organization. It is also a matter of determining the degree of decoupling one can afford and would like to have. There can be phases—for example, when markedly diverse expectations are placed on the organization, or during serious internal conflicts—when the organization's external presentation has very little bearing on its day-to-day reality. During other phases, such as difficult legitimation crises, it can become necessary to align the façade more closely with day-to-day operations within the organization, even if it entails a loss of flexibility.

In this respect, it would be naïve to view the external façade alone as the essence of things. By the same token, if one were to suspect that the primary motive for an organization's every decision lay in polishing its external image, one's picture of the organization would be a mere caricature (see Luhmann, 1964: 116). One can only begin to fathom the degree of decoupling and also gain a realistic impression of the organization as such once the external aspect, with all of its functionality, and the formal aspects, and in addition to that the informal aspects, have been fully understood.

CHAPTER 4

BEYOND THE ICEBERG METAPHOR: THE POSSIBILITIES AND LIMITATIONS OF COMMUNICATING ABOUT ORGANIZATIONS

The iceberg is a metaphor used in organizational research to illustrate that many aspects of organizations are hidden from sight. To the observer, only the tip of the iceberg, the organization's formal aspect, is visible, and even then one's attention is frequently directed to the areas that are lit by the sun, that is, the display aspect. The far larger part of the iceberg—the stances and attitudes of the members, the shortcuts they use, their informal day-to-day practices—lies below the surface and is barely recognizable to the external viewer.

The fascination the iceberg metaphor exerts is understandable. Because of differing densities between ice and seawater, only about one ninth of an iceberg's volume lies above the water line, while the better part remains concealed from sight. Since the portion of the iceberg below the surface can have massive extensions that are almost impossible to locate using technical resources, there is an unpredictability to icebergs that poses a grave threat.

FOCUSING ON THE TIP OF THE ICEBERG: DREAMING OF THE OPTIMAL ORGANIZATIONAL STRUCTURE

The image of the iceberg suggests that there is a tendency in organizations to perceive only the structures that lie above the surface. Such structures are particularly easy for observers to grasp because they have been set forth in officially accessible rules and regulations, organizational charts, and job descriptions, or have been specially conceived for ease of comprehension as is the case with websites, mission statements, printed materials.

One suspects that much lies below the surface and mounts an attempt—if it is at all technically possible—to raise the entire iceberg to the surface for the purpose of measuring, analyzing, and revamping it. Arguments between profit centers over resources, conflicts between departments over responsibilities, and complaints of divisional egotism within the business emerge and lead to demands for new forms of collaboration that entail "less friction." Or, a goal conflict within the organization may cause it to split into two separate entities, each with a single, unambiguous goal of its own.

Working with others on a day-to-day basis, which employees often find frustrating and tiresome, remains hidden from outside observers because it transpires below the surface. This can easily be set in contrast to the pretty picture of a streamlined organization that is free of contradictions. The organizational models that corporations, consulting firms, and sometimes even academics produce, be it lean management, the fractal enterprise, or the learning organization, represent the palette of colors every organization can use to paint a more or less specific picture of an alluring future.

Contrasting complex reality (the iceberg under the surface) with an attractive vision of the future (making the entire iceberg visible) no doubt has its charm. Since master plans, visions, and target conditions are simpler, more attractive, and make more sense than reality, which is perceived as chaotic, they can be used to develop what is termed "energy for change." Their good intentions are difficult to refute because they have not yet been subjected to the acid test, and they have their own particular appeal (Luhmann, 2000: 338).

As they are carried out, however, they lose their attractiveness. The more a given master plan is applied in concrete terms and implemented in the real world, the clearer it becomes that this concept, too, harbors contradictions similar to all the other organizational concepts known to date. The more a targeted condition is implemented, the more obviously the inconsistencies of the envisioned goal emerge. The more intensively lean management and business process reengineering models are implemented, the more clearly their blind spots emerge.

The organizations' process leaders, the participating consultants, and supporting academics may strongly oppose the crumbling of the master plans. The failure to achieve an ideal state is explained through error on the part of the personnel, employee resistance, a lack of discernment at the middle management level, or the incompetence of a certain consultant. The mantra is: the plan is good, but unfortunately the personnel aren't ready for it yet. The attribution of problems to individuals allows a master plan to be kept alive for some time. But ultimately it changes nothing about the basic problem addressed by the popular management adage: the more human beings proceed according to plan, the more effectively chance will strike. Organizations are constantly adjusting to changing conditions in their environment, but unfortunately seldom in the way the executives at the top would like (Luhmann, 2000: 346ff.). Experience shows that the iceberg one has raised to the surface with such great effort can quickly slip underwater again.

If bringing the entire iceberg into view on the surface is such a futile endeavor—amounting to formalizing all of the organizational structures—then which other options do we have for dealing with the inadequacies of corporate reality?

BELOW THE SURFACE: QUALITY CRITERIA FOR ORGANIZATIONAL ANALYSES

Using the iceberg metaphor allows one to signal that the self-portrayals an organization presents on its website, in its promotional literature, or PowerPoint presentations cannot be accepted without reservation. One expresses keen awareness that in addition to the colorful organizational mission statements (with their affirmations of customer satisfaction, integrity, and collegiality) there is a further reality that transpires beyond the procedural and operational manuals.

Yet the problem with the use of the iceberg metaphor is that it often misleads managers, consultants, and academics into *not* examining in detail the portion that lies below the surface. Standing in front of an iceberg picture that has been quickly sketched on a flipchart, they make abstract comments on relationships of trust, power processes, and the forms of communication that define an organization, without, as a rule, making the effort to analyze how each of these elements works in specific terms. They conduct a discussion of the attitudes, rituals, and taboos that are important for organizations in general but have difficulty identifying them in specific cases.

When the risks are assessed for an infrastructure project in the Near East, sweeping indications are made that "Arab tribal culture" could pose an obstacle to investment. When an investment project in Romania falls through, the reasons are described in shorthand as the "state-socialist mentality." But no explanations are forthcoming as to the specific way that "Arab tribal culture" or "state-socialist mentality" actually functions in the underlife of the business, government agency, or ministry in question. The use of the shorthand implies that other factors are involved, but no one makes the effort to discover exactly how these mechanisms operate. When the iceberg metaphor is invoked, the portions that lie below the surface often remain extremely vague.

The criterion for an accurate organizational analysis is the degree of precision with which the structures lying below the surface can be described. Harking back to our reflections on membership, goals, and hierarchies, the following are just a few of the questions that need to be addressed. How do the various motives for joining the organization (money, force, goal identification, the attractiveness of the occupation, and collegiality) interact with one another, aside from the lip service that members pay to them? What effects do goal conflicts have in the organization? While often escaping notice, how do goal shifts take place? And in which form are goals invented after the fact for the purpose of justifying actions? How do the power processes play out beyond the formal hierarchy? How are contacts with the environment, the possession of expertise, or control of informal communication channels utilized as trump cards in power games?

The challenge is not only to understand the structures below the surface, but to become aware of how they are linked to those that are visible on the iceberg above water. Which of the membership's motives can be satisfied through formal decisions by management, how can they be portrayed in the organization's external presentation, and how do they mesh with the motives that tend to stem from the organization's underlife? Which goals are suitable for presentation to the outside world, how can they be transformed into formal expectations of members, and which additional ancillary goals emerge that can only be communicated to the outside world with difficulty? As the different levels of the hierarchy interact, how do the surveillance of subordinates and the sousveillance of superiors affect one another, and what role does presentability to nonmembers play in the process?

It is only when we are able to answer questions such as these—and the image of the iceberg makes sense here—that we can understand the way a business, government agency, hospital, association, or university functions. And it is only when one has understood how the display aspect, the formal aspect, and the informal aspect interlock that one can grasp not only the individual aspects in themselves but also gain an overall impression of the organization.

Yet what is one supposed to do with these observations? How can they be put to use, inside the organization as well?

BRINGING HIDDEN STRUCTURES TO THE SURFACE: THE COMMUNICABILITY OF THE OBSERVED

It is very tempting to communicate about the organizational structures that lie below the surface. A newly hired employee, a consultant who has been brought on board, or the attentive, observant academic may exclaim, "I see something you don't see," and proudly report all the things that organizational science enables them to see below the tip of the iceberg, that is, below the formal structure and display side.

Yet the new employee, consultant, or academic who rises to the challenge of "identifying problems openly," "tackling thorny issues," and "addressing sensitive topics" will quickly encounter the organization's immunizing tendencies. An employee with a background in organizational theory, who claims that the success of a mining company does not depend primarily on its profitability but on acquiring political legitimacy at the state level, must be prepared that her CEO will consider her a suitable case for the company psychiatrist (Luhmann, 1989: 223). If a professor represents that numerous waves of reform have turned the university into a "planning monster" that is only held in check because the faculty is constantly breaking a host of often contradictory rules, she must not be surprised when her interpretation is indignantly rejected by the minister of education in charge of the reforms.

The impossibility of addressing structures that lie below the surface is referred to as "latent communication" in organizational science. Even if managers encourage their coworkers to "speak openly" and to describe their "real motives," the managers often expect the very opposite, namely, that the employees will be highly disposed to carefully maintain such communication latency (Luhmann, 1984: 459). Within a small circle of colleagues, a person might hint at one or another repeated infraction, or might inform the consultant confidentially over lunch about a company's "real balance of power" beyond the official hierarchy. But woe to the person who includes information of that kind in a note to the file, or brings it up during an internal conference with top executives—let alone mentioning it in a public statement. Raised eyebrows, outraged remarks from of all the other participants, or a sudden dressing down behind the scenes quickly make it clear to the individual what can be addressed and what is off-limits.

It must not be overlooked that communication latency fulfills an organizational purpose. In young marriages, a number of topics must be kept out of sight so that the fiction of consensus is maintained. And in cliques, it is impossible to openly discuss the weaknesses of every member if stability is to be maintained. In the same way, organizations have much that cannot be addressed candidly, in spite of all the demands for greater communication expressed in management literature. The danger of escalating conflict and losing legitimacy is too great.

For employees, consultants, and academics the art consists of sensing where, when, and how the vow of silence can be broken. Employees can utilize windows of opportunity to raise points that are critical of the organization. Consultants can see it as their job to discover organizational taboos and—at the risk of being removed—develop interventions that allow the organization to put their observations to use. Academics, whose primary audiences are not the organizations they are researching but their equally research-oriented colleagues, can ponder at what homeopathic dosages they can convey their insights. Even if it will never be possible to make every structure in the iceberg accessible, perhaps one or the other adeptly introduced revelation about protrusions under the surface will prevent a collision between the iceberg and a ship.

A SOMEWHAT LONGER JUSTIFICATION FOR A BRIEF INTRODUCTION INTO THE SYSTEM APPROACH

What constitutes a very brief introduction from a system theoretical viewpoint? Does it mean that the book can be read in one evening? Is it a book with barely more than a hundred pages? A book that costs so little that it's not even worth copying or printing out as a file at work? A summary of the current state of research—as compact as possible without allowing the author's own positions and discoveries to shine through too much? Or perhaps a book that focuses exclusively on one or two main thoughts?

This book is primarily directed at several constituencies: readers who have day-to-day contact with organizations as the members of companies, public administrations, universities, hospitals, political parties, non-governmental organizations, or the military; consultants who are attempting to spur the process of change in an organization; university students from a range of disciplines such as economics, psychology, sociology, anthropology, and labor science who want a quick and readily understandable, initial overview on the topic of organizations; and researchers who focus on organizations from a scientific perspective and are interested in learning more about the system approach to organizations. My goal was to provide these readers with a compact synopsis of the possibilities of organizational research from the perspective of the system theory.

Admittedly, for the author a very brief introduction initially entails painful decisions about what to omit. At this point, I would like to take a moment and candidly set forth the self-imposed concessions that characterize this book, the decisions I made concerning which perspectives to include, and in addition the distinctions one will be able to draw after reading this book.

Concessions

Our everyday perspectives on organizations are overly characterized by the dramatization of certain organizational phenomena as something novel. The dismantling of hierarchies, the training of intrapreneurs in organizations, or the networking of organizations—all of these topics are being introduced as new developments. Yet the fact is overlooked that fundamental change in the way organizations function requires decades, perhaps even centuries, rather than a mere handful of years. Thus, it is not difficult to dispense with a presentation of the latest trends in organizational fashion or the ones before, be it the concept of the knowledge-based organization, process management, or of new public management. If one has acquired a fundamental understanding of the way organizations work, innovative ideas—which often only *sound* innovative—can generally be classified quickly.

More painful by far is that this short introduction can at best only hint at the interesting development of the organization as a historical phenomenon over the last 500 years. It greatly enhances one's grasp of organizations to understand how they arose historically after individuals increasingly gained the freedom to make independent decisions about membership. In this introduction, readers with an interest in historical developments will have to content themselves with occasional fragmentary thoughts and references which will enable them to delve into the historical evolution on their own.

I have also forgone drawing systematic distinctions between different types of organizations. Readers may therefore be surprised to find a pharmaceutical company, a political party in a democratic country, and a wartime army cited as examples in the same paragraph. This automatically focuses attention on the commonalities between different types of organizations, although at the cost of differentiating between them. Nevertheless, I have introduced a number of distinctions—between goals, hierarchies, and memberships; between programs, communication channels, and personnel; and between an organization's formal, informal, and display aspects—and hope that this will make it easy for readers to investigate the differences between, say, a church and a corporation, a concentration camp and a school, or a university and a political party.

Likewise, this brief introduction does not undertake a systematic examination of the differences between organizations in different cultures. In that respect, dispensing with systematic differentiation between organizations in the USA, Germany, France, or Great Britain is not such a tragedy. The emphasis placed on cultural differences, particularly when it comes to the interplay between various organizations in the West, frequently serves only to conceal conflicts of a more fundamental nature. Rather, it is regrettable that I had no opportunity to discuss the differences between organizations in the Western world and those in Latin America, Africa, and Asia. At first, it is apparent that organizations have established themselves across the world. Almost every country—the structural similarity is obvious—has a ministry of education, a military, and businesses. Yet on closer examination, it is striking how differently these organizations often function. Focusing on decision-making autonomy with respect to membership, hierarchy, and goals can indeed sharpen one's eye for the particular features of organizations operating in the non-Western world, but this book cannot promise to convey an understanding of such special organizational phenomena.

Of greatest consequence, however, is that I have refrained from systematically elaborating on the various theoretical approaches to organizations. There are a number of very successful attempts at providing comparative introductions to the different theoretical perspectives of organizational research. Introductions to comparative theory offer the advantage of setting forth for the reader not only the complexity of the subject but also the complexity of the theoretical viewpoints. Afterwards, readers at best have different spotlights available that they can shine on an organization. Not infrequently, however, during the first exposure to a phenomenon, introductions that elaborate several perspectives result in confusion. Readers often find themselves wondering who is right. Thus, it is not only for reasons of brevity, but also to make the phenomenon of organizations easier to understand, that I have cast the material "from one mold." It is only in isolated passages that I have indicated the different perspectives brought to light by respective organizational theories.

The various academic disciplines—economics, psychology, sociology, administrative sciences, labor science, or anthropology—take different approaches to organizations. While it is true that they not infrequently reference the same classical thinkers and identical theoretical concepts, their perspectives frequently diverge substantially. That may be surprising, because the phenomenon to be described, the organization, remains the same. This introduction lays claim to serving as suitable entry-level reading for a range of disciplines.

Decisions

The claim of offering a *single* coherent presentation of organizations can be realized by forgoing a presentation that gives equal treatment to each of the individual theoretical and disciplinary approaches. The perspective from which my *particular* picture of organizations is drawn is Niklas Luhmann's systems theory. Even though organizational science sometimes displays an almost knee-jerk reaction against systems theory—much more so than among practitioners—it is nevertheless the theoretical perspective from which the specific characteristics of organizations can be described in by far the most precise terms. Here, systems theory initially means only that organizations are understood as social systems, which by virtue of their particularities have the ability to hold their ground in a world of at first unlimited complexity. Their special attributes distinguish them from other social constructs such as face-to-face interactions, groups, families, networks, communes, classes, protest movements, or even entire societies. Everything else, the purpose of organizations in modern society, the definition of their central characteristics such as goals, hierarchies, and memberships, and the differentiation between the three aspects of organizations, follow from the decision to understand them as social systems.

Within this *single* picture of organizations from the viewpoint of a systems theorist, I incorporate interesting theoretical insights and empirical examples from various theoretical schools. For example, the purpose rational theoretical approaches of Max Weber, Frederick Taylor, or Oliver Williamson are of interest to me in this book primarily because the external presentation of organizations frequently creates the impression that they are following purposive-rational models of corporate management. Neo-institutionalism plays a central role because it is a theory that allows us to understand with great precision the function that an organization's external presentation fulfills. As well, this book presents insights based on micro-politics and rational choice theory because these approaches allow us to explain—for example, when examining hierarchies—why subordinates sometimes exert greater influence on decisions than their superiors.

Naturally, to state that this book entails a *single* representation of organizations is to imply that they could also be portrayed in other ways. Depending on one's field or theoretical origins one might arrive at different descriptions, but then one has to argue over who has provided the more appropriate and applicable definition of the phenomenon. In the end, there can only be one "correct" view of organizations. In this respect, the disciplines and theories ultimately compete with one another over which portrayal, all necessary simplifications notwithstanding, best captures organizational complexity. I leave this assessment to the reader.

Differentiations

With all of its concessions, advance determinations, and decisions, this book still has far-reaching aspirations for a brief introduction. The idea is to use a systematic introduction of distinctions as a means of equipping readers with the analytical tools that will enable them to arrive at their own understanding of a wide range of different organizations.

Some of these tools address fundamental questions. How does the formulation of the terms of membership ensure that members comply with the organization's established purposes and hierarchies? Which aspect of an organization—the formal, informal, or the display aspect—emerges as recognizable in certain situations? How do these aspects interact?

Other tools tend to be suitable for answering individual questions that are central to a corporation, public administration, church, or university. How do the three formal structural features, namely, communication channels, programs, and personnel, facilitate and restrict one another? Which of the structural features are immobilized? Which informal expectations support or oppose the formal structure?

Still other tools are suited for micro-analyzing organizations. What is the primary factor motivating members of a department: force, remuneration, identification with purpose, the attractiveness of the activities, or collegiality? How do the means of motivation shift? How can work activity be programmed in terms of goals or conditions, and which program form is most appropriate in a given situation?

The systematic application of a number of differentiations in this book will allow interested readers to use it as a point of departure for further study. Especially the classical works on organizations—the writings of Herbert Simon, Niklas Luhmann, Michel Crozier, or James Coleman come to mind—are not easily accessible for the layman. Therefore, this introduction is also intended as an accompanying text for these often somewhat difficult books. If readers have a deeper and also theoretical interest, they can use the schema of the book, that is, its definition of an organization, its observations on membership, goals, and hierarchies, and on distinguishing between formal, informal, and display aspects, as a basis for reconstructing and comparing the ways such diverse theories as institutional economics, Marxism, micro-politics, or systems theory approach the phenomenon. Yet the book can also be used to run through the gamut of specialized organizational questions ranging from a central topic, for example, mergers, to supposedly secondary ones such as company parties.

In spite of its brevity, this book is also intended as a research tool that can be consulted time and again, even by individual chapter. It is secondary whether it is used to discover something surprising in the company where a person works, or to expose blind spots in a political party, a citizens' initiative, or an association in which one is active, whether it serves to prompt a question that leads to a brief academic paper of one's own, or provides consultants with a modest additional approach to client intervention. If readers begin working with the differentiations, gain surprising initial insights, and, hopefully, realize at some point that they must widen the scope of their reading, delve even deeper, and thereby render the distinctions even more productive, then this book will have proven successful.

Ideally, a book arouses interest in detailed description and more precise information about the origins of a phenomenon or about competing ways of viewing it. If this brief introduction leaves its readers with greater curiosity than before, the book will have fulfilled its purpose.

REFERENCES

Adorno, Theodor W. (1990): "Individuum und Organisation." In: Adorno, Theodor W. (ed.): *Soziologische Schriften 1*. Frankfurt a.M.: Suhrkamp, 440–57.

Allison, Graham T. (1969): "Conceptual Models and the Cuban Missile Crises." In: *American Political Science Review*, 63, 689–718.

Ashkenas, Ronald N., Ulrich, Dave, Jick, Todd and Kerr, Steve (1998): *The Boundaryless Organization: Breaking the Chains of Organizational Structure*. San Francisco, CA: JosseyBass.

Barnard, Chester I. (1938): *The Functions of the Executive*. Cambridge, MA: Harvard University Press.

Berliner, Joseph S. (1957): *Factory and Manager in the USSR*. Cambridge, MA: Harvard University Press.

Blau, Peter M. (1955): *The Dynamics of Bureaucracy*. Chicago, IL: University of Chicago Press.

Blau, Peter M. and Scott, W. Richard (1962): *Formal Organizations*. San Francisco, CA: Chandler.

Bommes, Michael and Tacke, Veronika (2005): "Luhmann's Systems Theory and Network Theory." In: Kai Helge Becker and David Seidl (eds): *Niklas Luhmann and Organization Studies*. Philadelphia, PA and Amsterdam: John Benjamins, 248–61.

Bosetzky, Horst (1974): "Das Don CorleonePrinzip in der öffentlichen Verwaltung." In: *Baden-Württembergische Verwaltungspraxis*, 1, 50–53.

Braverman, Harry (1974): *Labor and Monopoly Capital: The Degradation of Work in the Twentieth Century*. New York, NY and London: Monthly Review Press.

Brunsson, Nils (1989): *The Organization of Hypocrisy: Talk, Decisions and Actions in Organization*. Chichester: John Wiley and Sons.

Brunsson, Nils (2003): "Organized Hypocrisy." In: Barbara Czarniawska and Guje Sevón (eds): *The Northern Lights: Organization Theory in Scandinavia*. Malmö and Oslo: Copenhagen Business School Press, 201–22.

Burawoy, Michael (1979): *Manufacturing Consent*. Chicago, IL and London: University of Chicago Press.

Burns, Tom and Stalker, George M. (1961): *The Management of Innovation*. London: Tavistock.

Chandler, Alfred D. (1962): *Strategy and Structure*. Cambridge, MA: MIT Press.

Commons, John R. (1924): *Legal Foundation of Capitalism*. New York, NY: Macmillan.

Crozier, Michel (1963): *Le phénomène bureaucratique*. Paris: Seuil.

Crozier, Michel and Friedberg, Erhard (1977): *L'acteur et le système. Les contraintes de l'action collective*. Paris: Seuil.

Cyert, Richard M. and March, James G. (1963): *A Behavioral Theory of the Firm*. Englewood Cliffs, NJ: Prentice Hall.

Dalton, Melville (1959): *Men Who Manage*. New York, NY: Wiley.

Dreeben, Robert (1980): *Was wir in der Schule lernen*. Frankfurt a.M.: Suhrkamp.

Etzioni, Amitai (1961): *A Comparative Analysis of Complex Organizations*. New York, NY: Free Press.

Etzioni, Amitai (1964): *Modern Organizations*. Englewood Cliffs, NJ: Prentice Hall.

Festinger, Leon, Riecken, Henry and Schachter, Stanley (1956): *When Prophecy Fails*. Minneapolis, MN: University of Minnesota Press.

Freeman, Jo (1972): "The Tyranny of Structurelessness." In: *Berkeley Journal of Sociology*, 17, 151–64.

Friedberg, Erhard (1993): *Le pouvoir et la règle. Dynamiques de l'action organisée*. Paris: Seuil.

Goffman, Erving (1973): *Asyle. Über die soziale Situation psychiatrischer Patienten und anderer Insassen*. Frankfurt a.M.: Suhrkamp.

Gouldner, Alvin W. (1954): *Patterns of Industrial Bureaucracy*. Glencoe, IL: Free Press.

Gouldner, Alvin W. (1959): "Organizational Analysis." In: Robert K. Merton, Leonard Broom, and Leonard S. Cottrell (eds): *Sociology Today: Problems and Prospects*. New York, NY and London: Basic Book, 423–6.

Habermas, Jürgen (1981): *Theorie des kommunikativen Handelns*. Frankfurt a.m.: Suhrkamp.

Handy, Charles (1989): *The Age of Unreason*. Boston, MA: Harvard Business School Press.

Heydebrand, Wolf (1989): "New Organizational Forms." In: *Work and Occupation*, 16, 323–57.

Hochschild, Arlie Russell (1983): *The Managed Heart: Commercialisation of Human Feeling*. Berkeley, CA: University of California Press.

Hofstede, Geert (1993): "Organisationsentwicklung in verschiedenen Kulturen." In: Gerhard Fatzer (ed.): *Organisationsentwicklung für die Zukunft*. Köln: Edition Humanistische Psychologie, 327–48.

Hornby, Nick (2005): *A Long Way Down*. New York, NY: Viking.

Illich, Ivan (1975): *Die Enteignung der Gesundheit—Medical Nemesis*. Reinbek: Rowohlt.

Jackall, Robert (1983): "Moral Mazes. Bureaucracy and Managerial Work." In: *Harvard Business Review*, 5/1983, 118–30.

Love, John F. (1995): *McDonald's: Behind the Arches*. New York, NY: Bantam Books.

Lozowick, Yaacov (2000): *Hitlers Bürokraten. Eichmann, seine willigen Vollstrecker und die Banalität des Bösen*. Zürich: Pendo.

Luhmann, Niklas (1962): "Der neue Chef." In: *Verwaltungsarchiv*, 53, 11–24.

Luhmann, Niklas (1964): *Funktionen und Folgen formaler Organisation*. Berlin: Duncker & Humblot.

Luhmann, Niklas (1968): *Vertrauen. Ein Mechanismus der Reduktion sozialer Komplexität*. Stuttgart: Lucius und Lucius.

Luhmann, Niklas (1971a): "ZweckHerrschaftSystem. Grundbegriffe und Prämissen Max Webers." In: Niklas Luhmann (ed.): *Politische Planung. Aufsätze zur Soziologie von Politik und Verwaltung*. Opladen: WDV, 90–112.

Luhmann, Niklas (1971b): "Lob der Routine." In: Niklas Luhmann (ed.): *Politische Planung. Aufsätze zur Soziologie von Politik und Verwaltung*. Opladen: WDV, 113–43.

Luhmann, Niklas (1971c): "Reform des öffentlichen Dienstes." In: Niklas Luhmann (ed.): *Politische Planung. Aufsätze zur Soziologie von Politik und Verwaltung.* Opladen: WDV, 203–56.

Luhmann, Niklas (1973a): *Zweckbegriff und Systemrationalität. Über die Funktion von Zwecken in sozialen Systemen.* Frankfurt a.M.: Suhrkamp.

Luhmann, Niklas (1973b): "Allgemeine Theorie organisierter Sozialsysteme." In: Niklas Luhmann (ed.): *Soziologische Aufklärung 2. Aufsätze zur Theorie der Gesellschaft.* 2nd edn. Opladen: WDV, 39–50.

Luhmann, Niklas (1975a): *Macht.* Stuttgart: Enke.

Luhmann, Niklas (1975b): "Interaktion, Organisation, Gesellschaft." In: Niklas Luhmann (ed.): *Soziologische Aufklärung 2. Aufsätze zur Theorie der Gesellschaft.* Opladen: WDV, 9–20.

Luhmann, Niklas (1976): "A General Theory of Organized Social Systems." In: Geert Hofstede and M. Sami Kassem (ed.): *European Contributions to Organization Theory.* Assen: Van Gorcum, 96–113.

Luhmann, Niklas (1977): "Differentiation of Society." In: *Canadian Journal of Sociology,* 2, 29–53.

Luhmann, Niklas (1982a): "Ends, Domination, and System." In: Niklas Luhmann (ed.): *The Differentiation of Society.* New York: Columbia University Press, 20–46.

Luhmann, Niklas (1982b): "Interaction, Organization, and Society." In: Niklas Luhmann (ed.): *The Differentiation of Society.* New York: Columbia University Press, 69–89.

Luhmann, Niklas (1982c): *A Sociological Theory of Law.* London et al.: Routledge and Kegan Paul.

Luhmann, Niklas (1984): *Soziale Systeme.* Frankfurt a.M.: Suhrkamp.

Luhmann, Niklas (1989): "Kommunikationssperren in der Unternehmensberatung." In: Niklas Luhmann and Peter Fuchs (eds): *Reden und Schweigen.* Frankfurt a.M.: Suhrkamp, 209–27.

Luhmann, Niklas (1991): *Soziologie des Risikos.* Berlin and New York, NY: Walter de Gruyter.

Luhmann, Niklas (1993): "Die Paradoxie des Entscheidens." In: *Verwaltungsarchiv,* 84, 287–310.

Luhmann, Niklas (1995): *Social Systems.* Stanford, CA: Stanford University Press.

Luhmann, Niklas (1996a): "Membership and Motives in Social Systems." In: *Systems Research*, 13, 341–8.

Luhmann, Niklas (1996b): "Complexity, Structural Contingencies and Value Conflicts." In: Paul Heelas, Scott Lash, and Paul Morris (eds): *Detraditionalization: Critical Reflections on Authority and Identity at a Time of Uncertainty*. Oxford: Blackwell, 59–71.

Luhmann, Niklas (1997): *Die Gesellschaft der Gesellschaft*. Frankfurt a.M.: Suhrkamp.

Luhmann, Niklas (2000): *Organisation und Entscheidung*. Opladen: WDV.

Luhmann, Niklas (2002): *Die Politik der Gesellschaft*. Frankfurt a.M.: Suhrkamp.

Luhmann, Niklas (2003): "Organization." In: Tore Bakken and Tor Hernes (eds): *Autopoietic Organization Theory: Drawing on Niklas Luhmann's Social Systems Perspective*. Copenhagen: Copenhagen Business School Press, 31–52.

Luhmann, Niklas (2005a): "The Paradox of Decision Making." In: Kai Helge Becker and David Seidl (eds): *Niklas Luhmann and Organization Studies*. Philadelphia, PA and Amsterdam: John Benjamins, 85–106.

Luhmann, Niklas (2005b): "Allgemeine Theorie organisierter Sozialsysteme." In: Niklas Luhmann (ed.): *Soziologische Aufklärung 2. Aufsätze zur Theorie der Gesellschaft*, 5th edn. Wiesbaden. VSVerlag, 48–62.

Luhmann, Niklas (2010): *Politische Soziologie*. Frankfurt a.M.: Suhrkamp.

March, James G. (1976): "The Technology of Foolishness." In: James G. March and Johan P. Olsen (eds): *Ambiguity and Choice in Organizations*. Bergen: Universitetsforlaget, 69–81.

March, James G. and Simon, Herbert A. (1958): *Organizations*. New York, NY: John Wiley & Sons.

Marx, Karl (1962): "Das Kapital Erstes Buch." In: *MarxEngelsWerke. Band 23*, Berlin: DietzVerlag, 11–955.

Mayntz, Renate (1963): *Soziologie der Organisation*. Reinbek: Rowohlt.

Meyer, John W. and Rowan, Brian (1977): "Institutionalized Organizations: Formal Structure as Myth and Ceremony." In: *American Journal of Sociology*, 83, 340–63.

Meyer, Marshall W. (1979): "Organizational Structure as Signaling." In: *Pacific Sociological Review*, 22, 481–500.

Milgrom, Paul and Roberts, John (1992): *Economics, Organization and Management*. Englewood Cliffs, NJ: Prentice Hall.

Mintzberg, Henry (1979): *The Structuring of Organization: A Synthesis of the Research*. Englewood Cliffs, NJ: Prentice Hall.

Morgan, Gareth (1986): *Images of Organization*. Beverly Hills, CA: Sage.

Neuberger, Oswald (1990): "Widersprüche in Ordnung." In: Roswita Königswieser and Christian Lutz (eds): *Das systemisch evolutionäre Management—Der neue Horizont für Unternehmen*. Wien: Orac, 146–67.

Neuberger, Oswald (1994): "Zur Ästhetisierung des Managements." In: Georg Schreyögg and Peter Conrad (eds): *Managementforschung 4*. Berlin and New York, NY: Walter de Gruyter, 1–70.

Nordsieck, Fritz (1932): *Die schaubildliche Erfassung und Untersuchung der Betriebsorganisation*. Stuttgart: C. E. Poeschel.

Packenham, Robert A. (1973): *Liberal America and the Third World*. Princeton, NJ: Princeton University Press.

Parsons, Talcott (1960): *Structure and Process in Modern Societies*. Glencoe, IL: Free Press.

Peters, Thomas J. and Waterman, Robert H. (1982): *In Search of Excellence. Lessons from America's Bestrun Companies*. New York, NY: Harper & Row.

Pettigrew, Andrew (1979): "On Studying Organizational Cultures." In: *Administrative Science Quarterly*, 24, 570–81.

Reve, Torger (1990): "The Firm as a Nexus of Internal and External Contracts." In: Aoki Masahiko, Bo Gustafsson, and Oliver E. Williamson (eds): *The Firm as a Nexus of Treaties*. London: Sage, 133–61.

Rodríguez Mansilla, Darío (1991): *Gestion Organizacional: Elementos para su estudio*. Santiago de Chile: Pontificia Universidad Católica de Chile.

Roethlisberger, Fritz Jules and Dickson, William J. (1939): *Management and the Worker: An Account of a Research Program Conducted by the Western Electric Company, Hawthorne Works, Chicago*. Cambridge, MA: Harvard University Press.

Rottenburg, Richard (1996): "When Organization Travels: On Intercultural Translation." In: Barbara Czarniawska and Guje Sevón (eds): *Translating Organizational Change*. Berlin and New York, NY: Walter de Gruyter, 191–240.

Scharpf, Fritz (1993): "Positive und negative Koordination in Verhandlungssystemen." In: Adrienne Héritier (ed.): *Policy Analyse. Kritik und Neuorientierung. Politische Vierteljahresschrift, Sonderheft 24*. Opladen: WDV, 57–83.

Shils, Edward A. and Janowitz, Morris (1948): "Cohesion and Disintegration in the Wehrmacht in World War II." In: *The Public Opinion Quarterly*, Summer 1948, 280–315.

Sills, David L. (1957): *The Volunteers*. Glencoe, IL: Free Press.

Simon, Herbert A. (1957): *Administrative Behavior. A Study of Decision Making Processes in Administrative Organizations*, 2nd edn. New York: Free Press.

Smith, Adam (1999): *Der Wohlstand der Nationen*. Munich: dtv.

Spence, A. Michael (1974): *Market Signaling. Informational Transfer in Hiring and Related Screening Processes*. Cambridge, MA: Harvard University Press.

Strang, David and Soule, Sarah A. (1998): "Diffusion in Organizations and Social Movements: From Hybrid Corn to Poison Pills." In: *Annual Review of Sociology*, 24, 265–90.

Taylor, Frederick W. (1979): *Die Grundsätze wissenschaftlicher Betriebsführung*, 2nd edn. Munich: Oldenbourg.

Thompson, Victor A. (1961): "Hierarchy, Specialization, and Organizational Conflict." In: *Administrative Science Quarterly*, 5, 485–521.

Treiber, Hubert (1973): *Wie man Soldaten macht. Sozialisation in "kasernierter Gesellschaft."* Düsseldorf: Bertelsmann.

Ward, John William (1964): "The Ideal of Individualism and the Reality of Organizations." In: Earl F. Cheit (ed.): *The Business Establishment*. New York, NY: John Wiley, 37–76.

Weber, Max (1919): *Politik als Beruf: Vorträge vor dem Freistudentischen Bund. Zweiter Vortrag*. Munich; Leipzig: Duncker & Humblot.

Weber, Max (1965): *Gesammelte Aufsätze zur Religionssoziologie. Band 1*. Tübingen: Mohr.

Weber, Max (1976): *Wirtschaft und Gesellschaft. Grundriß der verstehenden Soziologie*, 5th edn. Tübingen: Mohr.

Weick, Karl E. (1976): "Educational Organizations as Loosely Coupled Systems." In: *Administrative Science Quarterly*, 21, 1–19.

Weick, Karl E. (1985): *Der Prozeß des Organisierens*. Frankfurt a.M.: Suhrkamp.

Weick, Karl E. (1995): *Sensemaking in Organizations*. London, New Delhi and Thousand Oaks, CA: Sage.

INDEX